The Covenant

Giving God the Reins

Kimberly Hicks-Graham

First published by Dog Ear Publishing
4011 Vincennes Rd
Indianapolis, IN 46268
www.dogearpublishing.net

ISBN: 978-1-4575-5931-0

This book is printed on acid-free paper.

Printed in the United States of America

1

Daybreak

THE day was breaking as I made my way down the very long, dark corridor to the select care area of the hospital. I had never heard of such a place before my husband, Glenn, was sent there, but I soon understood it was where patients were sent to rehabilitate. It was the place they sent all the people not well enough to leave the hospital, but well enough not to need full-time nursing. I probably had never heard of select care because they hid this section of the hospital in the corner with no nearby entrance. It seemed to me the best place for a morgue, not rehabilitation, but I am no architect.

I was there before the sun rose that morning because I wanted to catch the doctor while he was still doing his rounds. I planned this each morning, but rarely saw the doctor. It was almost as if he were playing a long game of hide and seek with me; I was always it and he almost always won. I needed to win that day, however. The night before had been long and hard on both me and Glenn, and I was so worn out I could barely stand the sound of my boots pounding the floor of the sad stretch of linoleum that lay between select care rooms. The sick color of the fluorescent lighting made my bloodshot eyes sting and shake in their sockets. I still recall the dullness of the lights, so dull that their light faded out before reaching the end of each of the ceiling tiles. I remember them because they reminded me of life: long periods of dark moments followed by bright springs of happy moments that instill faith once again. The darkness of the tiles made it seem that everything in the place had given up. I didn't like the thought of that. It made me more anxious as I walked toward the end of the hall in search of the elusive doctor. At the end of the hall I made the familiar left turn that opened to a long row of rooms. Very little sunlight made it through the small windows placed in the spare areas of the unit wherever they would fit. The entire area felt old and worn out. That feeling had leached into my being.

As I wandered down the hall, nurses passed me on their way in for the morning shift. They were fresh and ready for the day, relieving their tired and dreary colleagues whc hurriedly packed up to go home. I envied them for their ability to leave this place. It was all I wanted to do. Walking away from the nurse's station, I heard the haggard nurses sleepily telling the new arrivals the stories of the previous evening.

"Room 319 is going to need extra fluids today. She's been running a high fever. Be sure the doctor knows. 324 is going downhill too. Be sure to keep a close eye on him. 312 and 320 are making slow progress, but 320 is a little irritable, so watch out."

They never got to our room. I wonder what they would have said. "Room 302 seems to be getting better. We have no idea how, but he's just bounced back. It's a miracle if you ask me."

I passed a small Starbucks were doctors and nurses were standing around, they're smiling and making conversation. It was just another day for them, and Glenn would be just another patient. I heard a chuckle coming from the muttering as they waited for their grande lattes. The sound of laughter set me on edge. How could someone laugh in the midst of so much sadness? I fixed my eyes on the scarred tile beneath my feet as to not lock eyes with one of them. If I did, I knew they'd be able to see right through me. They would see the pain that was just below the surface. They were all smiling as they got their expensive cups of coffee; that was all it took for them to smile—a cup of coffee. The simpler times are what I missed so much. I missed the pleasure of drinking a cup of coffee. Since Glenn had been in the hospital, I drank coffee to survive another day. I had already forgotten what it was like to drink it in the quiet, calm of the morning. Glenn's sudden illness had changed so much about our lives—even the smallest things I had taken for granted for years.

When I got to the end of the select care unit and hadn't seen the doctor, I knew I'd missed him yet again. I looked on into the first waiting room is the ICU area. We'd been there and done that. When Glenn was first admitted for a sharp pain in his side that didn't seem to be getting any better, the ICU was our home. That is where we found out that the swelling in his abdomen and the searing pain in his side was not your run-of-the-mill infection. No, it was necrotizing factitious, the doctor told me. I had no earthly idea of what that even meant. It was hard to pronounce and something I had never heard of. Apparently is was also enough to send you to the ICU.

Looking across the tops of the heads of all the people in that room, I was glad to know we had moved on. Even if the select care unit was drab and depressing, it was at least a sign of progress. So many people were waking up in the ICU waiting room that morning after spending long nights in chairs and on couches, hoping for a chance to visit a loved one who had suffered some terrible incident—a heart attack, a motorcycle wreck, an aneurysm. I stopped for a moment and looked at the worried faces of parents praying for children who had come down with the flu but were only getting worse by the day. Some of the visitors had quilts and pillows on the vinyl couches. Fast-food wrappers lined the floor around their nested area. An elderly gentleman was all alone in a corner praying. I knew he was praying because I had done so much of it when I was in that waiting room. It was all you could do in that waiting room; pray for a miracle. Pray for mercy. Pray for God to heal what modern medicine could not. I recalled vividly the feeling of that waiting room, of the days and nights I spent doing the exact same thing alone and scared. My heart broke remembering those long nights. I was much better off than those people, frazzled as I was. I was grateful that I was no longer lingering nightly in that waiting area—grateful that Glenn was no longer a patient lying in one of those beds. I stopped and prayed for the families.

I had been alone for weeks at that point, except for the visits from our church family. Those weekly visits really raised our spirits. Glenn would light up every time they came in. He somehow never really talked about the gaping hole in his side or the rare bacteria that had sent him to the ICU in the first place. He didn't talk about when he would get out or his progress. Instead, he asked questions; he wanted to know how everyone was doing and how the church's new construction was going. Glenn was the head of the building committee and could hardly stand not to be at the meetings.

"How's the building coming along?" he'd ask every time a new face popped in. "You getting' along without the head tater?" Glenn was the type that always had to be in charge, so he had earned the name "head tater" from the building committee. They thought it was a kinder word for him than "dictator."

"All your tater tots and the mashers taters are keeping things afloat," everyone assured him.

"Hope no one's messing up too bad without the head tater there to keep you taters in line," Glenn would always say.

I loved to see him chatting like everything was fine, because I felt anything but fine. I was so tired—tired of being in the hospital, tired of waiting for the good news that Glenn would be released, tired of waiting on God to answer my prayer. I didn't say much about that though because I knew that would open the floodgates. Answering the simple question, "How are you today?" honestly could have been my undoing, and I knew that. I wondered if Glenn was feeling the same. If so, he was much better than I was at hiding it.

Watching my husband, who was living life day to day with no idea what would happen next, was both reassuring and alienating. *How could he be so calm and collected,* I wondered. Since he had been admitted to the hospital the month before, it had been nothing but catastrophic blows. First no antibiotic worked, then the pain got worse and his stomach swelled, so much I would ask him regularly when the baby was due to lighten the mood, and then the surgeries started. Day after day, it was always something new—some setback that kept us from getting on with our lives. The entire time, Glenn laughed and smiled. He didn't ask, "What are we going to do about the bills?" or "Why am I not getting better?" He simply took each day as it came. It gave me hope, but it also made me feel all alone. I felt I was the only one fighting the battle. I needed some sign that I wasn't alone. I needed Glenn to focus less on the bible study lesson and more on his health. I needed to know why everything was happening to us and when it would stop, but no one was offering any of those answers to me.

As I walked away from the ICU and back toward Glenn's room, all the questions I needed to ask the doctor swirled round my mind. I needed to make sure the nurses weren't over-medicating Glenn. We knew he had an addictive personality, so they needed to be very careful about that. Maybe that was why he was so nonchalant about everything—too many pills. I also needed to know what the plan moving forward was. Most importantly, I needed to ask when we could go home.

"Good morning, ma'am," a passing janitor mumbled to me out of habit. It may have just been a knee-jerk reaction for him, but it felt like a lifeline to me. It pulled me from my thoughts for a moment.

"Oh, good morning," I replied, lifting my eyes from the floor, the place they'd been trained on for what felt like months. My lips curled into a slight smile. A smile was almost more effort than I had to spare. I was saving all my smiles for the news that Glenn was being discharged. *Any day*, I thought. *It would happen any day.*

I looked down at my clothes after the janitor passed. What was I wearing? Everything was crumbled and seemed to hang off me. I generally dressed sharp, pressed skirts with matching blazers, a button-down shirt right out of the business professional section of the local department store. That day I was in wrinkled slacks and a shirt that was barely nicer than a t-shirt. I no longer had time to iron anything or put together a slick outfit. Some days I wore the same thing two days in a row because there was no time to do laundry. I dressed in the dark and put on whatever was easiest to get to in the closet that day. I was on autopilot, and even that was starting to give.

Tears stung the corners of my eyes as I realized I'd be wearing crumpled clothes for an indefinite amount of time. Glenn had made zero progress since we moved to the select care unit. I didn't understand why he was at a standstill. Why wasn't he getting better? I was praying nonstop for it. Was he not? He couldn't have been. That is what I began to tell myself. I was doing everything right, so Glenn must have been messing up. I had prayed day and night for God to help me change things. If things weren't changing, it was because of Glenn. But then there was the fact that even when he did finally get to go home, he'd never be able to work again. The infection had eaten into his muscle and his organs. He would never be the same. I had a good job, but we needed his income. Once we got out of the hospital, we would lose everything. And then the medical bills would start pouring in. The light at the end of the tunnel wasn't looking so bright.

"Good morning, Mrs. Hicks," the night nurse said to me as she extended her arms to hug me. She was heading out for the day. I leaned toward her to fall into her embrace, but I pulled myself back before she could wrap her arms around me. Any more emotion than that would start the tears, and I couldn't afford to lose control. I smiled and patted her arms. The other nurses looked at me from their places at the nurses' station. I forced a smile and walked on toward the room that had become my second home.

All our nurses were friendly, but that morning they seemed to be especially attentive. I had gotten to know them well from our daily small talk. I could feel their eyes on me until I reached the door and disappeared into the room with HICKS written in big, black letters on the door. Inside the room was a dry erase board that listed the names of the nurses and doctors on duty. The janitor had even added her name to the board.

Whoever wrote the board would put little happy faces or flowers around their names and titles. It was one of the many ways the staff tried to make patients feel good. They did these little things to make the place bright and cheery. I appreciated their effort, but they all got to go home at the end of their shifts, and we would be left to figure out the days ahead. *Trust in the Lord with all your heart, and lean not upon your own understanding and he will direct your path,* I thought as I looked at a purple and yellow flower on the board. I had tried that, but the days and nights in that depressing hospital room were wearing on me. I was losing my sense of direction, so I worked harder to find it. I prayed more, and I insisted Glenn pray more too.

"Did you write anything last night?" I asked him as I scooted my chair closer to him.

"Nothing last night," he told me.

I had been giving him a notepad every night and asked him to write down what the Lord was telling him when he prayed. Every day that I returned, the page was still blank. This is how I knew he wasn't trying hard enough. God would show him something if he asked.

"Did you pray?" I asked. "I think if you did a little more we'd see some change."

"Baby, you know I pray," Glenn told me. "Always, baby." When he looked at me I could see how worn out he was. His eyes looked a little dull and his cheeks sallow.

"God hasn't come through yet, but He will," I told him, watching the door for the chance the doctor would come in to tell us some good news finally. "We've come a long way, you know. I just walked by the ICU and it reminded me that where we are now compared to where we were is amazing. Your recovery is going to blow us away! It's going to be our testimony," I insisted. Glenn smiled weakly at me.

"You're my warrior," I said to drown out the quiet in the room. I was telling myself that as much as I was telling Glenn. "You know you've got that deep-water faith in the shallow-water end of the pool."

"Thanks, baby," he told me, placing a hand on mine.

I was frustrated that he wasn't praying hard enough to have anything written down when I came every morning, but I knew that he had *big* faith. Because of that, I also knew that God would save him. His faith was deep, and he was steadfast. That was all we needed. We had been through hell, we had been climbing a mountain I truly wasn't expecting, but we would have a testimony at the end. I could already see it. I just needed Glenn to get better. I needed a miracle. I needed God to finally show up. I'd kept my end of the deal; I needed Him to keep His.

As I stared down at the blank notebook Glenn was supposed to be journaling in, a night nurse named Joanie popped her head in and said, "We have been reading Bible verses tonight, and I think he stumped me a little."

"Oh yeah?" I asked, my eyes shooting over to Glenn. I had grown fond of Joanie, and I knew Glenn had too. She was bright and she had a warm presence that filled the room. When Joanie was there, I felt like things were going to be okay. "Glenn stumped you with scripture?" I said, raising an eyebrow. Glenn wasn't the type to rattle off Bible verses. He read the Bible, to be sure, but he wasn't one of those people who throw out verses just because. He also wasn't the type to quote a Psalms or a Gospel just to let people know he knew his Jesus. Glenn was quietly faithful. Showboating wasn't his style.

"You look a little surprised," Joanie replied, cocking her head to one side and training her eyes on me.

"Glenn is always full of surprises, isn't he?" I joked.

"He sure is," she agreed. "Surprised me last night with a request for a chicken sandwich at midnight."

"He didn't!"

"He did," Joanie quipped back.

"And Joanie made it happen," Glenn added.

"Of course she did." I smiled. That was Joanie. She just made things happen. But I wanted more than a chicken sandwich at midnight. I wanted—I needed—a sign that things were getting better. It was the one thing she couldn't deliver, as good as she was as a nurse.

"Did he tell you?" Joanie asked me, her smile fading a little.

"Tell me what?"

"About the blood," she said. "We have ordered another scan of his stomach this morning. Oh, and don't be alarmed if he says things today that really don't make sense. His potassium is very low, which can make someone say strange things."

Things hadn't made any sense since we arrived at the hospital one Wednesday afternoon, so I was getting used to things not making sense. I peeked over at Glenn. He was twisting a piece of the hospital blanket in his large hands and I could see the outline of his jaw muscle his teeth were clenched so tightly. It was a look I wasn't used to from my easy-going cowboy. I imagined the look was a result of the fuss everyone had been making over him. Glenn was an understated kind of man; he didn't look for attention. In fact, he avoided it. Having visitors stopping by and flowers sent every other day was taking its toll. It was reminding both of us that he was sick, and everyone knew it. Problem was, I could not accept it. I looked at one of the get well soon cards I had placed on the window sill of the hospital room and scoffed. I was tired of waiting for him to get well soon. It was time to do it, already. Glenn just needed to cowboy up and get better.

I turned my attention back to Joanie as she continued to tell me the news from the evening—news Glenn never offered willingly—news that I had to get from others because when I asked him how his night had been, he inevitably shrugged, flashed a weary grin and said, "It was fine. I'm in good hands here."

"His sugar level is also low, lower than he can sustain for any length of time. We have ordered shots, and they will sweeten him right up!"

I giggled. When it came out, I recoiled. A giggle? I hadn't done it in ages. I looked at Glenn, and he giggled too. So did Joanie. It lightened the mood for a minute. I felt like I had just come up for air after being under water for a month. The air felt good, but strange. How had we made it to a place that laughter felt so foreign?

"Soon I will be so sweet. I'll give you a big ole kiss to prove it," Glenn told me, his voice a little slurred. He looked at me and winked. Butterflies flitted around in my stomach and I was up for air again. The room got brighter—maybe my pupils swelled in response to that wink—a wink I knew so well. It told me that he would be fine, and there was my sign. *Oh, Kim, always looking for a sign.*

"Yes, you will, and you sure can, buddy," Joanie said with her throaty chuckle.

A friend came in as we stood smiling at one another. She was there to check in, on me as much as Glenn.

""Hey there, Julie," Glenn said as she poked her head in the door.

"Well, look at this," she said as she set her purse on the floor beside mine. "It looks like a party is going on in here. This is a nice change of pace." She hugged me and I melted I her arms. The looser I got, the tighter she squeezed. When we finally stepped back from the embrace, she smiled at me and said, "You look great today, Kim." I knew what that meant. I didn't look so wound up. I looked happy.

"How's Three in the Saddle going without us?" I asked. Glenn and I were in a marriage bible study with my Julie and her husband, Bill. We always had dinner either before or after and talked about the study meetings.

"It's great, as always. But we are ready for y'all to come back. We're missing our favorite couple. Bill misses having you to talk at afterwards," Julie joked. "I told him that if it's three in the saddle, he should be able to tolerate going with just his wife."

"We're certainly riding three in the saddle right now," I sighed. Julie's cheerful smile turned to one of pity, and like that my head was back under the water. Thinking about our bible study was another quick reminder that we were missing out on life, and Three in the Saddle had become a foundation for me and Glenn before he got sick. It worked from the idea that as you marry, you saddle up and ride with your partner through the hills and valleys of life. What is so important is that you aren't just riding together, you ride with God, so three in the saddle—you, your spouse, and God. We had grown so much as a couple going to the studies, and we had also grown close to Julie and Bill. They were anchors, and people that we both agreed we loved spending time with. Glenn was different than me, so sometimes we disagreed about what constitutes a worthwhile friendship (he still hung out with some drinkers and wild cards, which I never was too fond of). Bill and Julie, however, we both enjoyed.

"What are you up to this morning, Miss Julie?" I asked to move the conversation into something less bleak.

"I thought I'd come see y'all to see if you needed anything. I got your folks back home safe and sound, so I'm going to be out running some errands," she said in her soft-spoken drawl. Julie wasn't just there to see how we were doing; she had taken a vacation day from work to get my parents home from the hospital. My dad had fallen ill and was admitted to the same hospital as Glenn for a few days. When he was released, there was no one to drive him. He was in no shape to drive, my mother had no license, and I couldn't leave Glenn. So, Julie volunteered to be our chauffer. "I mean that. I'll be out and about getting some supplies for our next ladies' organization meeting and for a charity auction I'm helping put together, so whatever you need, I'll be somewhere to get it."

"Girl, you are always buzzing around," I said. "Just thinking of all the things you do exhausts me."

"It doesn't feel like work though, it's so much fun," Julie insisted. "I think it helps remind me of how fortunate I am. It's easy to forget that in the hustle and bustle of life."

"Ain't that the truth," I agreed. "I don't know that I've said many thank yous lately with all this going on."

"That's more than understandable, Kim," Julie assured me. "You have a lot on your plate. And that is why I mean it when I say, tell me what you need!" Julie gave my arm a little pinch. She was usually not so assertive.

"I know you mean it," I told her. "I don't know what we'd do without you."

Julie blushed a little and said, "Hush. You'd do the same for me."

"I think we're good. The only thing I need right now are some answers and for this man to get better," I told her, looking at Glenn. Just then the nurses came in to do his dressings.

Answers were scarce and scary when they came. We still didn't know how Glenn got necrotizing fasciitis to begin with—that terrible disease that ate a person's flesh. It had been painful and ugly, and it required a surgery called debridement procedures every four days. The doctors had created a gaping hole on his left side, about three inches by six inches to be exact, to drain fluid and remove any tissue that had infection. Because the bacteria spread so quickly, the debridements kept Glenn alive, but they also put a constant strain on his kidneys and liver, the latter of which was not in good shape to begin with. Glenn had contracted hepatitis C from using dirty needles decades before. You see, Glenn had developed a serious drug problem while he was serving in Vietnam. This made both the procedures and the drugs that they had to give him for pain doubly difficult. Glenn was a former addict with a shot liver and a propensity to become addicted to any and all narcotics. This is what made me so frustrated. Glenn had overcome his past—given up drugs and drinking, and now he was in a situation that he needed drugs to treat the pain from this terrible disease. My question was, why? Why would God give us this kind of test? It seemed cruel. After all he had been through, with the war and the addiction, and overcoming addiction. Why throw him into this now?

The one bright spot in all the medical conundrums we faced was the Glenn somehow did not seem to be in much pain, until it was time to change the packing that in the wound. Every day I had to watch as nurses stuffed him with large pieces of black gauze and then wrapped him like leftovers with a plastic cover that looked like saran wrap. As they did this, a vacuum hose ran from his side to keep air going into the wound and drainage coming out. When those times came, he couldn't just grin and bear it. Those sessions required a healthy dose of morphine. Every single time it happened, I watched the possibility of him becoming addicted inch up.

"It's that time again," the nurse on duty said. Glenn tried to smile at her. I moved to my chair on the right side of him where I always sat during the dressing changes. "You know the routine."

Glenn rolled over to expose the hole in his left side. I grabbed his hand as one of the nurses began unwrapping the plastic. His grip tightened with every pull, then the morphine hit and he relaxed a little. His palms were sweating, or maybe it was mine. I looked over at the nurse and I saw inside my husband's body. I squeezed his hand as I watched wads of soggy, black gauze came out of his side. I looked down at Glenn, as I always do. He was silent. His chest rose and fell in slow, rhythmic motions. I tried to ignore that the person being worked on was my soul mate to appreciate how precise and amazing the procedure was. The nurses have it down to an art.

"You're doing great, Mr. Hicks," the nurse said as she worked diligently, never looking up.

"Call me Glenn," he managed to say.

The nurses finished with the debridement and another nurse arrived. Her scrubs are a different color—a dull grey, plain and strict. Standing beside the nurse with hot pink scrubs on, I guessed the new one was the nurse in charge. She moved toward Joanie and talked quietly to her and no one else. As she spoke, I watched Joanie. She shook her head as the woman talked to her. I could have sworn I saw her eyes glaze over before she looked down to the floor.

"We are moving to the lower level," the head nurse announced. She spoke with authority; there would be no discussion on her orders. Any and all questions were prohibited. She continued, "He needs more care, and we have a nurse specialist downstairs. She is waiting for us, so let's get packed up to move now."

Wait, what?

I just stared at the woman, waiting for some further explanation. I looked over at Glenn for a moment, and he was doing the same.

"We are going *now*," she said, and began preparing Glenn to move.

Joanie and the head nurse began unlocking the wheels beneath the bed. As they worked, they moved wires and cords to Glenn's lap so they wouldn't catch in the wheels. I began folding up blankets and picking up slippers and socks. Julie was still there, thank God, and she started gathering vases of flowers that sat around the room. As I worked to get all my clothes into a bag, the nurse rolled Glenn out of the room. I stopped being neat and started shoving everything I could into the bags. She was leaving with my husband, with or without me.

Out in the hall, I look down toward the ICU and mutter, "Here we go again." We were off to another floor. I wondered how long we'd be on the next one.

The nurse wheeled Glenn down to an old elevator marked "staff only" and pushed the down arrow. Almost immediately the bell rang out its high-pitched tone, and the door opened. Two nurses maneuvered the bed and all the machines and charts into this dreary elevator. There was no room for me. The nurse in charge shot an icy stare at me from the other side of the elevator door and snapped, "There are stairs just on the other side of the door. We will see you downstairs."

With that, the elevator began to close, swallowing Glenn. I saw him disappear behind the cold, metal doors, but just before he was gone completely, I heard words that sent me spinning into a new level of consternation—a level that I would not escape for some time.

"We need to know, do you want to be resuscitated if you code in this elevator? Do you have a directive on file?"

From a two-inch crack, those words came clear and harsh. Her voice sliced through me. What was worse, I didn't hear Glenn's response. The doors closed, leaving me locked out. I was severed from the most important exchange my husband would ever have—cut off from him in such a real way that I almost felt something break inside me.

Code in this elevator? That meant die. Glenn could die. That did not make sense. Nothing had, but that I could not process. He was going to be fine. That was the plan. We were going to get back to bible study and church and life. Coding in the elevator was not in my plan. It was neither miraculous or a testimony. It was all wrong. Everything was all wrong. My world had spun out from under me. I was free-falling. I couldn't get hold of anything. I was just dropping into an oblivion. I had lost every bit of control, and to that point in my life, I had been in control of everything.

I knew Glenn wouldn't know how to answer the question. He needed me for help, but I wasn't allowed in the elevator. I learned in a flash that life doesn't always change slowly. Some of our biggest moments happen in a matter of milliseconds.

I had arrived at the hospital that morning thinking about all the setbacks Glenn's sickness has caused. I wondered what I was missing at work and how much trouble I I'd be in for missing yet another day. I worried that my boss would lose patience with my situation. I glowered at the sight of the hospital—a hospital I had been in so much that I knew every mark on the floor, every crack in every tile, every bulb that needed changed or that hummed louder than the others. I knew every doctor and every nurse by name. All I could see was what *I* was missing. My perspective changed in a heartbeat.

Standing on the other side of an elevator listening to a nurse ask my husband if he had a directive on file made all those other things just evaporate. *Am I in a nightmare?* We had done everything the right way, all according to God's plan. I followed all the steps, checked off all the boxes. I had done all I need to do to keep myself from being on the other side of elevator doors with those words ringing in my head.

Most importantly, I had already *told* God how I saw all of this turning out. I saw great things. I *knew* great things were coming. So why was I standing there brokenhearted? Why was the entire universe moving forward while I'm stuck in a downward spiral? Why were *we* there? Why was my faith being tested again and again? I had proved myself. What more did God want?

"We have been obedient; now it is time for us to receive our reward. We have been waiting on you, Lord. Why aren't you giving us a miracle we can use as a testimony?" I begin to whisper, standing next to Julie outside that awful elevator door. "We're supposed to have testimony reflecting on your amazing grace and how our faith in You caused an impossible recovery that could only be of You. Think about what we have been through! This story will change someone's heart! Lord, do you hear me? Are you listening?"

I stopped and looked down at all the cards and the bags. We were just supposed to be moving floors.

"Oh, Julie, did you hear what she said?" I gasped. She looked at me, her eyes wide and soft, and nodded. Her lips stayed pursed tightly.

Panic swelled inside me as I stared at the dingy elevator door. *How could they not let me go with my husband in a moment like this?* I wondered. *It's just protocol!* I decided. *That's it. They have to ask everyone that question when they move them. Yes! That is it! We will have our testimony!*

The light went out as the elevator sunk to the floor below. Julie and I took off down the hall for the stairs. We kept running when we hit the stairs, our arms full. I was shocked when we made it to the floor with everything still in our arms. We darted into the main area on the floor, silently. The only noise we make comes from our panting. I had no time for words. I needed to find Glenn.

We made it to the bottom floor before Glenn. Julie and I stood silently and waited for the elevator doors to open. I stared so hard at the doors that they began to wave in the morning sunlight. Seconds moved like lifetimes. I looked away and noticed a bouquet of fresh flowers lining the nurses' station. Someone was celebrating a special –maybe a birthday or anniversary. They came to work that day and received beautiful fresh cut flowers. Whoever the flowers belonged to was having a wonderful day, each bouquet a reminder of how much they were loved and needed. I looked back to the elevator and held my breath. I needed to see Glenn's face again, but he was nowhere in sight. I heard a woman's laughter as I searched the halls for him and the small team of nurses.

"I am a lucky girl," I heard a woman say behind me. I disappeared for a moment and returned back to those happy times for me—the times when life was full of possibility and hope, not fear. The time before an elevator door shut me out of my husband's life.

2

Blind Date

"**TERESA,** I don't think it would be a good idea for me to go. It's my birthday; I need to spend it with my family."

"Come on, Kim! You'll have fun. You deserve a night out for your birthday."

"A night out is one thing. This is a blind date. I do *not* want to go on a blind date with you. Seriously, it isn't a good idea," I insisted.

"His name is Glenn Hicks, and you're gonna love him. Trust me!"

Teresa was a car dealer I had gotten to know through work. I liked her immediately, and eventually our business transactions led to a friendship outside of talking car loans. Teresa started inviting me to go to car auctions with her, sometimes for the entire weekend, and before long we were having dinner or going to a movie a couple times a week. Teresa was my age, but our lives were nothing alike. I was shy and introverted, always on the insecure side. In short, no one has ever described me as the life of the party. Teresa, on the other hand, was the kind of person whose presence is always known. She was outgoing, adventurous, and always had a good story to tell about some crazy thing that happened in Rome or Athens or, who knows where else. A single mom of two boys, my life and the stories that came from it were no match for Teresa's. To be honest, I was always a little jealous of her. I loved my life and being a mom, but she seemed to have everything. For Teresa, life was an adventure. For me, life was a series of scheduled events; it was paying the bills, meeting deadlines, and getting to practices on time. I was grateful, but a little boring.

"You know I am usually more than willing to join you on your little outings—God knows you are the most interesting person in my life—but I just don't see me having fun this time. Dating is hard enough. A blind date? No thanks."

"Don't you always have fun with me?" Teresa insisted. I couldn't deny that I did. From the time I met her I wanted to be her friend in hopes that I might catch some of the fun she was having. I was fine with just being in the wake of the fun she was having.

"Of course I do, but that is when it's *us*. I'm not interested in spending my birthday with some stranger that will probably wish he were doing something else. I don't even have a sitter lined up. Remember, we're not all able to decide to do things on a whim," I teased. Teresa was unencumbered. She had nothing keeping her in one place, and so she might just decide in the moment that she wanted to take off for California for a couple of days, and off she'd go. She was a free spirit that went where the wind blew her. I both admired and was anxious by her lifestyle. A weekend away for me meant three months of planning and preparation.

"Can't your ex keep the boys? You know he never minds extra time with the boys."

"I know he'd be fine with it. I just hate to take off on my birthday like that."

I knew that my ex would have no issue at all keeping the boys so I could go on a birthday getaway. Our marriage had ended as amicably as a marriage could, and he was an active and loving dad, and always helped me when I needed it. Really, it was less about my boys and more about me. Meeting new people was never my strong suit. In fact, I hated it. I was never a social butterfly, and after having kids I found my children the perfect respite to all the social events adults are generally expected to attend. They gave me a reason to stay home in my sweats instead of going out to happy hours or to the new nightclubs in town.

I may have envied Teresa's life in some ways, but I was used to mine. It was comfortable for me. It was structured and predictable—both of these are pluses in my book. I was a in a bit of a lifestyle limbo when it came down to it. There was a part of me that really wanted to spread my wings and fly with Teresa, but I had no idea how to do that or if it'd be worth it in the end, and I always have to know how things will work out before I start. I wanted controlled chaos, I suppose. I wanted adventure, but I needed it to be calculated and safe. That is kind of my trademark.

"Worst case scenario, me and you have a blast and leave the men in the dust. Best case scenario, you meet a good-looking man on your birthday and have a blast. Notice you're having a blast no matter what," Teresa pushed.

"Fine, fine, fine." I finally gave in. Teresa had never let me down before. *Why not?* I thought.

'Perfect! We'll leave for Tyler Saturday afternoon."

Tyler, Texas was a town about an hour from Longview, where I lived. Tyler is no Manhattan, but there is much more to do there than in Longview, and for me it was like a mini-vacation.

Saturday at about two Teresa showed up in her brand-new convertible Mustang. The top was down and the music was blaring. I loaded my bag in the trunk of the little sports car and off we went.

"Tyler will never be the same!" she giggled as we hit the road.

"Top down is the only way to travel!" Teresa repeated as we drove. The whole ride down I fought with my hair and squinted at the wind that hit me. I gripped my purse like it might fly out at any moment. She'd laugh when she looked over at me trying to keep hair from my eyes and out of my lipstick.

We arrived at the Holiday Inn in Tyler forty-five minutes after we left. I mentioned that Tyler is an hour from Longview; that was only when someone other than Teresa was driving. As she pulled into the parking lot, I flipped the visor down and popped the mirror open to check my hair and make-up. Wow. The wind had taken its toll. My hair was a tangled bird's nest and my nose and cheeks were red from the East Texas sun. I frantically ran my fingers through my hair trying to tame it and then began digging in my purse for my powder and lipstick.

"Let's do this, lady!" Teresa exclaimed as she circled the lot looking for a place to park near the entrance.

"I have got to get my face and hair under control. I can't go in looking like this," I said, scowling at what I saw in the mirror.

"We'll freshen up in the room," she insisted. I flipped the mirror closed and looked at her. She was also windblown and sun kissed, but she wore it with confidence. Teresa looked like a Bohemian goddess with her messy hair and worn makeup. I, on the other hand, felt like a sunburnt circus clown. I couldn't introduce myself to someone looking that way. Conversation was hard enough for me. I couldn't be distracted by the fact I knew I looked like a vagrant. I made a last attempt at smoothing my hair and applied a coat of lip gloss before I finally got out of the car.

I was silent as Teresa eased her car into a parking spot. She chattered on about something, but I couldn't hear her over my racing thoughts. I had to map out what I'd say. I needed a plan before I went in there. I went through my introduction in my head three times before the car was in park. I tried not to think about what I looked like.

"You ready to meet your date?" Teresa asked.

"I don't know how you talked me into this," I mumbled back.

"It's gonna be fun!" she said, winking at me.

I started scanning my surroundings. Where was this mystery man? Teresa told me he was gorgeous, but that was all I knew. *Was he too good-looking for me? What would his face look like when he saw me? What if I could see the disappointment. My gosh! Why did I agree to this?* My thoughts ran wild. As they did, I felt the fight or flight instinct kick in. I glanced around the parking lot, but soon realized trying to escape was futile. I was already in Tyler, so there was no going back.

My heart pounded behind my ribs as I tried to talk myself off the ledge. *It's going to be fine,* I assured myself. *It is just one night. You can do this. If it doesn't go well, who cares?*

As I worked on taking deep breathes, a tall, slender man with salt-and-pepper hair appeared at my door. I looked up at him as he opened the door for me. My eyes immediately dropped. I was thankful for my sunburn all of a sudden. It was hiding my blushing. I noticed his cowboy boots as I looked down. They were nice—ostrich I think. I began to lift my eyes. Pressed Wranglers and an impressive belt buckle. He was handsome already, and I hadn't even seen his face. When I finally worked up the courage to look at his face, he eased his cowboy hat back and said, "Hi. Don't worry; I won't bite. You can get out—promise."

"Thanks," I replied, my voice almost a whisper "I'm good." Those were the only words I could get out. I struggled to say something else—anything. But that was all I could muster. All that planning I did, and my words wouldn't come out when I needed them.

I waited for the look of disappointment on his face, but instead he smiled. It was then that I caught my first look of beautiful blue eyes. They were bright and brilliant with curiosity, and they were locked on me. I felt his gaze go right through me. It worked its way through every part of me. Suddenly my heart sped up again. I was convinced he could see how terrified I was. *God, what is he thinking?*

"Well, yes, you are looking very good for sure. Now let's get you out of this car."

It was a quick save on his part. *Focus, Kim,* I told myself. *Get out of the car.* As I stood up, I realized how tall he was. I am 5'3", and he towered over me. As my hand disappeared inside his palm, I felt the sweat from my palm. I knew he felt it too. I waited for him to recoil, but he didn't miss a beat. He kept a firm but gentle grip on one hand and used his other hand to help lift me from the car. My skin tingled beneath his touch.

I was smitten from the word *go*. I looked over at Teresa, who was grinning as she watched me make a fool of myself. She was as cool as a cucumber on her side of the car, as usual. There was no blushing or reaching for words for her. Just unbridled confidence, and a wicked little grin as she watched me.

"Glenn Hicks," he said when I was finally out of the car.

"I'm Kim." My words came out in awkward jerks. Speaking had become foreign to me suddenly.

"So nice to meet you, Kim." He smiled and my stomach flipped around inside me. He was out of my league, but didn't notice or didn't care.

"David's inside," Glenn told us as he grabbed our bags from the trunk. David was my date's baby brother.

The lobby was cool. Inside, Teresa introduced me to David. He looked exactly the way I had imagined him. Teresa always showed up with tall, handsome men that looked like they had money. David was both tall and handsome, and the Presidential Rolex he had on his wrist told me he also wasn't hurting for money. He was sharped dressed, like his brother—alligator boots and matching belt, topped off by a custom cowboy hat. I looked at the two gorgeous man standing side-by-side and a giggle almost escaped me. We had hit the jackpot. It was then I realized how we looked in contrast. I fought the urge to smooth my hair again. As we stood there with them, I wished desperately that Teresa didn't have a convertible. I was windblown, sunburnt, and salty with dried sweat, as I met the most gorgeous man I'd ever been out with.

David was an expert auctioneer in high demand for estate, auto, and exotic animal sales. After introductions, he and Teresa went out to look at a car David was selling the next day at an auction. That left Glenn and me alone to get to know each other. My pulse skyrocketed when they first walked away, but within a minute I was at ease. We had no trouble talking, just the two of us. Let me rephrase that; he had no trouble talking. Glenn just started and didn't stop. Being shy, I was fine with that. The sound of his voice calmed my nerves. He was also very funny, which helped.

In the time it took to look at David's car, Glenn must have told me everything about his life. He talked about his tour in Germany during Vietnam and made it all the way up to what he had for lunch on the way over to Tyler. I found out he had been a world traveler, and he truly enjoyed experiencing life. He talked a little too much, but he was interesting, not to mention a real looker. As he told me all about his trips to Europe, I listened attentively as I flipped my hair and kept readjusting my shirt. He was so gorgeous, and I was so, disheveled.

When Teresa returned, we headed up to our rooms. The men followed us, and again I became hyper aware of my appearance. I wondered what I looked like from behind as I walked in front of this good-looking stranger. I lifted my shoulders a little higher than usual and straightened my back as much as I could. *This is so much trouble,* I thought as I nitpicked my every move. *Do I really want to continue with this date?* Then Glenn's eyes flashed across my mind and I realized, *Oh, yes, I do!*

Teresa and I got to the rooms the Hicks brothers reserved for us and I was impressed yet again. It was spacious and nice. It could have been any dumpy room in East Texas at that point, and I would have been fine. I just needed to shower and fix my hair. I didn't care about the amenities. But it was a good sign that the place was nice. Good-looking man, good-looking place. *Maybe Teresa was right about the blind date,* I thought as I stepped into a hot shower.

That night I was decked out in Teresa's clothes. I didn't have the wardrobe she did, and if I wanted to keep up with my date, I needed something nicer than my usual. I slipped into a pair starched jeans and a starched button-up. Teresa was smaller than me, so the fit was tight. I felt a little like I was in someone else's skin.

"Stop fidgeting!" Teresa hissed as I waited for her to finished getting ready. "And for God's sake—smile!"

"Thanks, Mom," I mocked as I tried to keep my hands still.

As she finished curling her hair, she asked me a laundry list of questions.

"What did you guys talk about? Do you like him? What is he like? I think he likes you!"

"We just returned to grade school!" I joked as she quizzed me about Glenn. "It's like we're getting ready for a homecoming dance." I was waiting for her to slip me a note: *Do you like Glenn Hicks? Check yes or no.*

"I just want to know what you think," she replied, putting a hand on her hip.

'He's great," I told her.

We went to bar called the Black Stallion to dance that evening. David dropped us off at the door. Teresa and I walked in together and were met with loud music and cloud of cigarette smoke. I looked at Teresa to see if she was as put off as I was, but she looked like a fish in water. She was looking around the place for a table. I took a deep breath and thought, *When in Rome.*

As we stood looking around, I was startled when I felt a hand rest on the small part of my back. I snapped my head backwards to see who was touching me, and my heart skipped a beat when I saw it was Glenn. He was pointing me toward an open table. My breath caught in my throat. He was touching me. His touch was light, but I knew it was there. It was the sexiest thing he could do: just touch the small of my back to guide me the direction he would like to see me go. With a gentle touch and firm direction, Glenn showed me right where I needed to go. *Happy birthday to me,* I thought to myself.

Country tunes blared across the bar and had couples all over the dance floor doing the traditional Texas two-step, everyone adding their own little moves. When "Cotton-eyed Joe" followed a slow song, couples parted and everyone started line dancing. It had been years since I had been to a dance club, but nothing seemed to have changed since my exit. There were cute little girls dressed up in perfectly starched jeans and shirts wearing belts with lots of sparkles and boots that cost several hundred dollars. They were all hooked up with cute, young men with perfect bodies and killer smiles, their jeans so starched that you wondered how they even got their legs in them. Everyone did their best to impress, dancing and drinking as they got to know each other, or at least tried to get to know each other enough for one night. *They have so much to learn about life,* I thought with a grin. *That cute little cowboy looks good but is probably out for one thing only!*

Any other day I might have been jealous of those cute, little girls with those strapping young guys, but not that night. That night I was ruling the world.

"I am going to make my way to the bar for drinks. What do you like?" Glenn asked. The music was so loud he had to lean down to my ear. His breath tickled my neck as he talked.

"Surprise me," I said. " I like anything."

"Surprise you?" he asked, his head coked to the side.

"Yeah!" I smiled.

The truth was, I had no idea what I wanted. I didn't really drink, so I had no idea what to tell him. I was more accustomed to Chuck E. Cheese than I was honkytonks. I hadn't had to choose an alcoholic beverage for ages.

He removed his cowboy hat again and said, "Yes, ma'am. I shall return." He placed his cowboy hat on my head and disappeared into the crowd. When his salt and pepper hair was out of sight, my anxiety surged. How would he ever find me in the crowd? Would he just leave me there and find another woman—someone as beautiful as he was handsome? Then I remembered, I had his hat! He left me his hat! I wondered what that meant. It occurred to me when Glenn returned he had left his hat so he would be able to spot me in the sea of heads, most of which stood taller than my own.

Sitting there without him was excruciating. The music seemed louder and the smoke heavier. Seconds moved by like hours. Without Glenn there, the place started getting smaller and less appealing than it had been even when I first walked in. I considered reapplying lipstick, but didn't want to miss him coming back, so I just sat perfectly still; I didn't dare touch the hat.

After a significant amount of waiting, I began to wonder if he had taken off after all, hat or no. *He was too good for you, Kim,* I told myself. *What did you expect?*

When I finally saw those bright blue eyes making their way toward me, I relaxed. Glenn was sporting a massive grin and held a drink in each hand. There were people all over that bar, many beautiful people, but I saw no one but him, and I felt confident that he saw no one but me that night.

"Jack and Coke," he said as he handed the drink over.

"Great! One of my favorites," I said as I grabbed the drink. "Good choice."

I took the first sip of a Jack and Coke I had never had and pretended I had reunited with an old friend. When I had a drink in the past, they were always something fruity, pretty, and frozen. Occasionally at a dinner I would have a glass of wine, but frankly nothing ever tasted great, so I just stuck to iced tea most of the time.

"You always use the stir straw to drink?" he asked with a sly grin.

I didn't get the joke, so I just nodded and continued to suck my drink through the stir straw as if that was how you do it. As far as I was concerned, I was doing great.

"Do you want to dance?" he asked.

"Yes," I said. And dance we did.

He was very good, and I got a chance to touch him. His belt and his starched jeans felt so good. He touched my shoulder as he moved me around the dance floor, guiding me with a gentle touch. The evening just kept getting better. It was the best birthday I could remember.

Two drinks and many turns on the dance floor later, I was feeling a bit lightheaded. I found our table and sat down. It was sticky from spilled drinks. I needed to go to the bathroom but had no idea where it was or how I'd ever find my way back. I couldn't see over anyone to find our spot again. I took a quick glance, and I saw no arrows pointing the way back to me.

"Would you like to come with me to the restroom?" Glenn asked. It was like he read my mind!

"Yes, yes, I would like to go with you."

I wanted everyone to see me with this tall, sexy man. Look at who I am with, girls. I win! I followed the smell of his cologne through the smoky bar. As we walked he would brush up against me, and I would feel my cheeks burn.

The evening was magical, but soon the music was off and the lights were on. We all stepped outside. It was a very cool evening for late May. I could smell cigarettes on my clothes. As we all stood in the cool air and chatted, I couldn't focus on the conversation because I was thinking about the way the night would end. I knew this was a one-time thing. He was out of my league in every way. So it was soft kisses, and we were headed back toward Longview very late. Top up! XXXXX

3

Puppy Love and Then Some

THE next morning Glenn called me. And the morning after that, and the morning after that. Every day he called me. He called to say good morning, or to ask how my day had been. Every time I answered the phone and heard his voice, I was shocked that he had called again. And every time I hung up the phone, I feared, and expected, it to be the last time I would hear from him. *I'm just a little fling,* I thought. *He's going to find a woman who is as gorgeous as him and cut me loose.* I tried to prepare myself for the day he disappeared. The only problem was, I was in love—head over heels in love.

As I waited for the clock to finally strike midnight and my coach to turn into a pumpkin, Glenn failed to show any signs of sneaking out of our budding relationship. In fact, phone calls stopped being enough for both of us, so we plotted out ways to see one another. He was in Killeen, four hours away from me, but still we found ways to sneak in spare moments. I would ride along with Teresa to the auctions we knew David worked, and Glenn would tag along with his brother when his schedule allowed. I had never enjoyed going to car auctions so much in my life. Every time I saw him, I felt everything inside me catch fire.

"Hello, beautiful," he'd say, and I'd become a lovesick teenager.

Being with Glenn was like a little vacation for me every time I saw him. We weren't doing anything spectacular—generally we spent our time sitting on his tailgate outside of car auctions people watching—but every moment with him was magical. As we sat outside in the June sun, we laughed at the characters that wondered into the auctions and shared stories about our past. It was on a tailgate that I learned a lot about the man I was falling deeply in love with.

Usually the stories we shared were lighthearted. We told one another about embarrassing moments and laughed about how stupid we had been when we were young. As we got more comfortable with each other, our stories would get more serious from time to time. It was during a mild July evening that Glenn told me a little about his experience in Vietnam.

"I got a little carried away over there," he admitted. "I experimented with a lot of different kind of drugs. I just got caught up doing what everyone else seemed to be doing. I did more than some, but less than others. I am not proud of that, but the truth is, lots of the guys over there used drugs. I was one of them."

"I'm sure it wasn't easy," I replied.

"It sure wasn't. But I went too far. I hope this doesn't make you think differently of me—" he paused and looked off in the distance and then said, "It just kind of got away from me. It started as partying with the guys to try to forget where we were, but it quit being a party. I'd shoot coke for a pick me up and then smoke pot to bring me back down. I'm not proud at all, but that's the truth."

For the first time since I first met him, I didn't know what to say to Glenn. I had never really known anyone that had been a drug addict, especially not *cocaine*. I looked at him and tried to imagine him as an addict. I just couldn't do it. I couldn't picture this handsome, classy cowboy sticking a needle in his arm.

"That is in my past though—a long, long time ago," he assured me when I didn't say anything. "I haven't gone near anything like that in decades. It was another time and place, and I was a different person, you know what I mean?"

"I know," I finally sighed. I could see by how well put together Glenn was that he wasn't the same person. "I don't care about your past. We were all different people then."

Most of our conversations were less intense than that one. Most of the time we sat on that tailgate of a truck was spent laughing and flirting. The evenings were just right. Not hot or cold, and for June and July in Texas, those evenings were unheard of. I wouldn't have cared if it were 110 degrees outside though. I was in heaven.

When the tailgate rendezvous weren't enough, I started staying at Glenn's when my boys were at their dad's. We talked just as much there; the only difference was we didn't have to say goodbye when an auction came to an end. Once we stayed up talking all night. The next morning, we went straight to a nearby bakery and bought fresh, hot donuts. We ate almost all of them before I finally said goodbye. I think we were both full after two; we just didn't want our time together to end. It had to, though. I had work that day and so did he.

The four-hour drive from Killeen to Longview became a regular trek for me, as we carved out our love affair. There was life outside of our love story though, and that made things tough sometimes. I had a job and two small children. The reality was I couldn't just get swept up in Glenn; I couldn't run away on a whim and throw responsibility to the wind. Running away every chance I got may have felt like freedom for me, but I knew it was unfair to my boys.

"I can't keep leaving the boys," I told Glenn during one of our sleepovers.

"You have to live your life too, baby," Glenn insisted.

"I just feel so guilty when I leave," I said, biting on my thumbnail.

"You're a great momma. You shouldn't feel guilty. But if you need to spend less time here, I understand," Glenn assured me.

I just couldn't do it; I couldn't spend even less time with him. It was hard enough only getting weekends with him. I knew losing those would kill me. So, I came up with a plan that would help me not to feel so guilty. I had the girls next door as my weekend babysitters. They were fourteen and sixteen, and the boys loved both of them. They always loved watching the boys, too, mainly because when they were at my house, they could stay up late and play games with the kids. I would buy pizza, pull out the sofa sleeper, and rent a few movies. Every weekend felt like a big slumber party for the boys and their babysitters, and I got to get my Glenn fix. Life was great. I had solved my mom guilt.

Weekends became as exciting as Christmas to me. All week I looked forward to Friday—to the day that Glenn would wrap his strong arms around me. He was so amazing. It didn't take long for me to imagine being married again, to Glenn. With one failed marriage in my past, I knew exactly what I wanted this time around, and it was Glenn. I'd spent years with a man that I never felt a real strong connection with, so I was ready to be with a man that made my life feel like something special every day. I knew from my past marriage that when there isn't a spark, it just won't last. There was nothing huge that caused our split—there was no infidelity, abuse, or neglect. We just grew apart and couldn't find our way back to one another. After the divorce, and even before it when I knew divorce was where we were headed, I racked my brain trying to figure out where we had gone wrong. After meeting Glenn and understanding love in a whole new way, I realized that my ex and my marriage may have been cursed because we were never really on the same page to begin with. I saw a post to one of the social media sites that simply states: "Rowing your boat harder doesn't help if you are heading in the wrong direction. Sometimes you are just going around in circles." That summed up my situation with my ex perfectly.

Our marriage just kind of quietly dissolved. I was too young to understand then that marriage was a covenant. I saw it as a contract that can be broken when the fun is gone or a person gets tired of working for it, not as a promise to God. It was a contract I'd signed, and so when the fire was gone, I broke the contract. This time, I understood marriage differently, but I also felt differently. I knew that with Glenn, the fire would never go out, for me, anyway. I just hoped that I wouldn't screw it up. Truth be told, I had no idea how to enter a marriage or what to do once you were in one, though.

I had spent my life watching my parents in a combative marriage. I don't know what they felt like, but from the outside it looked like nothing but a struggle. There was no joy or closeness—just drudgery, every single day. I assumed that was how all marriages ended up. My parents seemed to resent one another and were always unhappy with their life, so every bump in the road to them was overwhelming. They had no foundation in their marriage, and by foundation, I mean God. They lacked the harmony that people are able to find when they allow God to be the ultimate leader of their heart and home, and that was my model for marriage. I guess it made sense that I left my first marriage so easily.

As I matured a bit and began to meet other married couples, I began to see that married folks for the most part *were* in love and happy. I also began to see that they worked at their happiness and let their commitment get them through the rough times. Instead of driving a wedge between them, hardships made them even stronger and more in love. That wasn't how it worked in my home. I saw kindness and hand-holding. I saw people telling each other they were in love with the fact that they were in love, and love wasn't assumed or taken for granted; it was shown in words and actions. I wanted that life. I had failed at my first marriage, but I just knew that Glenn and I could have that life. I *knew* it.

"Good luck finding a man now," my mom scoffed when I told her I was getting divorced. "You have a lot of baggage. You should have just stuck it out."

"I wasn't happy though, Mom," I told her.

"Welcome to marriage, Kim," she hissed. "You stay in a marriage whether you like it or not. It's what you do, Kim."

Despite my mother's warnings that no man would want to be saddled down with my baggage (or her grandchildren), I held out hope that I'd get another chance. When I met Glenn I was pretty sure he was my second chance. I wasn't going to be so naïve about what a relationship was or required my second time around. This time, I'd make sure I was making a promise not just to Glenn, but also to God, which meant that come hell or high water, we'd work out whatever hit us. And, I have to say, Glenn made it pretty easy to want to work for a relationship. In so many ways, he was the man of my dreams.

"You just got divorced, Kim!" my mom exclaimed when I told her that I thought I'd found my soulmate. I may have been on cloud nine, but she was always there to bring me back down to earth.

"We didn't *just* get divorced," I rebutted, rolling my eyes.

"You should never have ended your marriage in the first place!" she spat.

"Well, I did, Mom."

"Yes, you did. And it hasn't even been a year," she reminded me. "You've already got some strikes against you. Do you really want to rush into something else that could end in another divorce?"

"The next time I marry, it'll be the last, mother."

"We'll see," she barked.

My mother has been miserable in her marriage for as long as I could remember—not because my father was awful, but because she was a miserable person in general. There was no way to make this woman happy, and so naturally her marriage was a far cry from a fairy tale. I was convinced that she was most angry at me because she had stayed in a miserable marriage when I had gotten out of mine. She created her own prison, though. First, she was destined to be unhappy no matter what because she chose unhappiness. There was also the fact that to her, divorce meant failure. It was that black and white. You get married, you stay married, no matter how difficult a marriage was, anything was better than divorce—and love had nothing to do with it. Unfortunately, since she saw marriage as a life sentence rather than a lifelong commitment, she didn't feel the need to work through problems. She just let them fester and poison the relationship. I believe one of the reasons my mother was such an austere figure was that she had been raised with six brothers and sisters during the post-depression era. Her dad died of black lung disease when she was just a child, making life extremely difficult for her family. Life made her heart and her personality hard. She became so hard from her upbringing that I never once remember my mother laughing or saying "I love you" to anyone, including my father.

Some women lean on their mothers as a support system when they go through a divorce. I, however, felt myself crumbling under the weight of her judgment as I went through my divorce. Suffice it say, I was collecting plenty of demons from my mom's criticism about the way I was living my life. I left my husband because marriage wasn't quite what I had expected, and marriage for my mother was less about finding Prince Charming (but she lucked out with my dad, he was a wonderful prince) and more about doing what everyone does—grow up and get married. I never heard her talk about her and my dad's love story. She would just say how hard she worked during the time he was off in Korea during the war, making a home for him when he returned. She always said how hard she worked and sacrificed to make a home and have a family. In other words, she didn't need love and romance; she only needed a way out. Her heart and feelings had little to do with her choice to get married or to stay married for sixty-plus years. I guess because she came into marriage under those circumstances, she was not receptive to anyone who lived life differently or demanded different things.

I didn't need my mother's support. I knew Glenn was the one for me, and no one would spoil that for me. By the time I met him, I fully understood that my divorce had not been the right thing to do—that I had walked out when I should've stepped up, but the fact was I did it, and there was no going back. We had a cordial divorce, and I started the next chapter in my life, just me and the boys. Their happiness became my focus, and it seemed to me that I was accomplishing that. I knew that even if I had not made my marriage work, I was doing all I could for the boys, and I deserved to be happy. I felt like a success in my heart no matter what my parents or anyone else thought. I was, and am, to this day, passionate about the choice I made. I wasn't going to live with guilt. God forgave me, and I finally forgave myself and was ready to move on. As ready as I was, I was still caught off guard when it came to a head.

I had just gotten in from mowing the lawn, so I was sweaty and a little sunburnt. I was just about to hop in the shower when the phone rang. Usually I'd let it go, but I decided to answer it really quickly. After all, there was someone whose call I was always waiting on.

"I have news; I am relocating to Longview." A rush of words came from the other end of the phone before I could get hello out.

"Hello? You are what?" I replied.

"Sorry, hi," Glenn said quickly, backtracking to what should've been the beginning of the conversation. "I am moving to Longview; you heard me right. I got the job I've been waiting on, and I am coming in this coming Saturday."

I was sitting on the floor of my bedroom leaning against the bed with my foot on the wall. I looked down at my shorts and legs, still covered in grass. I thought about how I really shouldn't have been by the bed with grassy, dirty feet. I was also sweaty and covered in dirt. I knew leaning on the white wall was going to leave a mark. The concern came and left in an instant. I didn't care about anything except the words I just heard. Glenn moving to Longview meant we could be together more often. That wasn't all though.

"And I think I am in love with you," he added.

"I think I love you too!" The words just came pouring out of my mouth. I love you too; it seemed so natural.

By the time I hung up the phone, I had forgotten all about taking a shower. Hot, sweaty, and covered in dust and grass clippings, I stood in my bedroom with tears of joy running down my face, cutting through the grime that lawn mowing had caked on my cheeks. I rushed to my friend's house to tell her that someone did love me. I couldn't just keep that kind of news to myself! I wouldn't call my mom just yet. Why ruin the moment?

XXXXX

4

The Fairy-Tale Life

GLENN moved to Longview to trailer house in a small, shabby subdivision that bordered the Lake O' the Pines. I would go over there in the evenings after work with the boys. He worked twelve-hour days, so gathering furniture for the musty, old trailer did not go quickly. The house consisted of a bed, a blowup mattress, a kitchen table with a leg so wobbly the table had to be propped against the wall, and an old couch, but I didn't care one bit. Every evening we were there, gathered around the wobbly table like a real family.

In the nights after the boys were asleep on their air mattress, we would talk about our previous marriages and why they didn't work. We realized that we had similar experiences; in both our marriages, we were going in a different direction than our partners and that ultimately caused the demise of the partnership. Although we talked a lot about our previous marriages (him especially), we never really talked about the possibility of a new one together, and that was all I could think about. He was amazing and I wanted to be his wife, but he was in unchartered territory and it intimidated him.

"I love you, but I've never been with someone like you and I just don't know how it will work," he told me.

What he meant was that I had a much calmer lifestyle than he was used to. I didn't drink or go to bars. I raised my boys, and that was about it. As time passed, though, I guess he started to see how it would work. We took the boys to VBS, went out to dinner, or just took a drive around the lake in my very unhip minivan (which was actually better than the clunker he drove that was called "the rig car" because it could handle the lease roads he always had to drive down). He began to see what life was like without bars and late nights, and he liked it. No, he loved it. And so it was time . . . to meet the family.

"We've got our family reunion coming up. I'd like you to be my date if you don't have any plans," Glenn said to me with a smart, little grin.

"I think I can make time for that," I replied, smiling ear to ear.

Meeting Glenn's family was as amazing as I had imagined. I loved them all. They were so loving, and they made me feel like a part of the family right away. I was waved over into all the family photos, even though I insisted I shouldn't be included.

"I'll just be the photographer," I told them. "I'm not a member of the family."

"Yes, you are!" his mother argued. "Or you're going to be anyway!"

It was then he finally said the words I'd waited for since he moved to Longview. On the way home from the reunion he looked at me and said, "You know, we should get married. I feel like that would be the best thing for us. I want to be a dad to the boys. Let's talk to them. What do you think?"

"Heck yes!" I blurted. Usually I prayed on big decisions, but I didn't pray that time; I just knew. I didn't need direction or counseling; I had everything under control. When you know, you know, and I knew. So did Glenn. We both realized that from the outside it probably looked like we were moving fast, but we were certain about what we had, and anyone that knew and loved us could see that there was no reason for us to wait to tie the knot.

"You just better remember to show up, Kim!" Glenn told me as we marked our calendars –*November 24: Getting*

Married! "You have a couple of months. I bet you'll change your mind about me before then."

"Oh, I don't think you need to worry about that," I assured him, and then I kissed him to make sure that he knew how very serious I was. I had never known that kind of love in my life. There was no way I was going to let that go.

"Me and Glenn are getting married!" I announced to my mom and dad once we decided that November 24 would be the date that we said 'til death do us part, and really mean it.

"We're so happy for you, sweetheart," my dad said. "And we love you."

"No, *we* are not and no *we* don't," my mother corrected him, her arms crossed over his chest. "She's making a mistake and hurting us! Why would I be happy about that?"

"Well mom, too bad. I am doing this and I shouldn't have to defend my decision to be happy," I told her.

"We'll see how long *this* lasts," she mumbled. "We'll see when the new wears off if you feel the same." I could have engaged her, but I knew that was what she wanted so I ignored her. This wasn't about her or her misery; it was about me and Glenn, and no one was going to dampen my excitement, not even my mother.

On November 24, we stood before a few close friends and our children and vowed to love each other for the rest of our lives. The wedding itself was much smaller than my first had been, but the vows I knew were so much bigger. Everything felt different this time. Looking at Glenn in his cowboy tuxedo as I recited the words after the pastor, I saw into our future. I saw us growing old together. I saw it all in a way I never did with my first marriage. This time, when I uttered my vows I said them not just to Glenn; I was also making a covenant with God, and I knew that. Granted, I had the butterflies in my stomach when I looked into those blue eyes of his, but there was something more than that too. This was puppy love and then some. Contrary to what my mother believed, what I had with Glenn wasn't going to fade. My love for him wasn't fleeting, and I knew that with God in the center of our marriage, it would only grow stronger with time. This wasn't a fairy tale; it was something much more powerful.

We danced as a husband and wife that day, and I felt like the most beautiful woman in the world. Glenn did that. The way he looked at me that day, and every day, was constant reassurance as to how he felt about me. I never once wondered if Glenn thought I was beautiful. He told me often, but even if he didn't, the way he looked at me always did. I had gained about thirty pounds in the time we were engaged, which generally sent me into a self-loathing spiral, but with Glenn in my life, I almost didn't notice the weight. My whole life I had struggled with both my size and my self-image; I would cram myself into jeans three sizes too small that would eventually make me sick they were so tight so I wouldn't have to admit my size. Glenn had a way of making me forget about that extra weight though; he made me feel good about myself. When he hugged me, I would disappear into his long arms. That was the safest place in the world. And whenever we went out, I knew that no other woman existed to him; it was only me. Having a man like Glenn think you're the only woman in the world does wonders for your self-esteem. My cowboy was the total package, and he was MINE.

December came, and cold weather crept in to East Texas. Glenn was working on a drilling rig nearby, which was extremely hard work, even when the temperatures weren't torturous. I assumed it was miserably cold working out in the field, but he made it look easy. He worked twelve-hour shifts then came home and helped with dinner or breakfast, depending on what time he got home from his shift that day. What a life, my life—my pretty little life. The only thing not perfect about it was my anxiety—my fears about what Glenn might be doing. There was a guy he carpooled with every day to and from the work site, and I knew that the guy was a drinker. He was the type that liked to stop after work and have a few, and I knew this about him. Every time it was his turn to drive, I would start calling the second I knew they were headed home. I'd call every half hour or so of their two-hour drive just to make sure Glenn didn't stop and drink.

"Hey, babe. How was work?" I'd start out—an attempt

to mask my surveillance behind a simple, little check-in and 'hello.'

"About the same as always," he'd tell me. I'm sure he knew I had motives beyond finding out how his day went, but he always played along. He humored me.

I'd go on to tell him what we were having for dinner that night. I might even use dinner as an excuse to check in again.

"Do you mind grabbing a red onion on the way home?" I'd ask. I could go get the onion, but it gave me a reason to call in and make sure he wasn't at a bar. It wasn't that I didn't trust Glenn; I did. I just also felt the need to protect him—to shield him from all the baggage his past brought with it. I knew that for Glenn one drink was too many and a thousand wasn't enough, so I wanted to help him avoid the little traps and pitfalls that he might stumble into. That meant not only did I check in when he was with his carpool buddy, but I also kept a close eye on anyone that he hung around. I saw life being a certain way. With Glenn as my husband, everything was finally perfect. I had to make sure that no bad apple snuck in and spoiled our perfection.

Our first Christmas together proved to me that I really did have a perfect life (and the perfect man), and it also validated all the work I did keeping Glenn on the straight and narrow. Glenn invited my ex to come to the house early Christmas morning so when the boys woke up, all their parents would be there for the super Santa unveiling (I say all because Glenn had already accepted my boys as if they were his own). When he suggested the plan, all I could do was smile. I thought quickly about my mother and her warnings that no man would want my baggage—a woman with an ex-husband and two kids—and I thought about how very wrong she was. Glenn not only loved me despite my "baggage"; he invited my "baggage" right into our home for Christmas morning so my boys would have all the people they loved most—their mom, dad, Glenn—with them as they opened their gifts.

We continued to have my ex over for major holidays and birthdays. He and Glenn got along wonderfully, and the boys loved having everyone there for all their special days. Neighbors thought we were crazy; we knew they talked about us because the kids would mention things they heard when they were playing outside. I cared about as much about what they thought as I did what my mother thought. It worked for us, and my kids knew how much they were loved. If my mother had taught me anything, it was how to ignore the naysayers in your life and do what you heart tells you is right. I can at least thank her for the thick skin she helped me develop in the face of judgment. How's that for glass half full?

Glenn took the boys to school every opportunity he could. The boys loved the change from Mom to Mr. Glenn, a term of endearment they came up with when Glenn and I started dating and they called everyone they met "mister" or "miss." The name stuck, and so did Glenn. I loved watching them drive away together each morning. Glenn would call out, "Bye, Mom! Have a good day! We love you," waving all the way. The boys would be all bundled up in their coats and gloves, hauling backpacks full of books. They smelled of waffle syrup and orange juice. What happy times. And to make things even more perfect, the boys and I got more than just Glenn in our family. There was also his daughter, Lacie Shane Hicks, who was graduating from high school when we met. She had lived with her dad most of her early years, but left to be with her mom when she was a teenager. When I met her, she had blossomed into a beautiful young lady, ready to finish high school and start college. *Beautiful* is the perfect way to describe her, inside and out. The first thing you notice when she walks into the room is her beautiful blue eyes—bright, just like her daddy's—and long, blonde hair. She has a smile that you cannot help but smile back to, even if you've had the worst day of your life. Every time she came to visit, we were complete.

Some families have trouble blending, but ours seemed to come together fairly easily. The boys loved Mr. Glenn and I loved Lacie. I particularly enjoyed sitting back and just watching she and her dad. They were so much alike it was uncanny. They chuckled and smiled just the same, and they also share triple-jointed fingers and toes. Lacie was the female version of her dad, to be for sure. She was also the daughter I never had, even if I did get her later in life. I loved having another girl to talk to and shop with. The boys always protested any kind of shopping, but Lacie was rearing and ready to go. Our time together was always precious, and we packed as many things as we could into each visit, especially after she finished high school started at University of Kentucky, or Kentucky University, as Glenn would say.

"U of K, Dad, not KU! They are not the same school!" she would always correct. Glenn would just wink, his blue eyes sparkling.

As the boys got older, we found ourselves involved in every activity our small town had to offer. We raised pigs for FFA, marched in the band, ran track, and played Little League baseball and football. I was washing uniforms round the clock when we weren't out at games or livestock shows. The school was small but competitive, so everything we did, we did all the way. One year on Thanksgiving weekend we had a playoff game. It was thirty-five degrees and raining, but there was no way that we were going to cancel. Lacie was in town on a break from school, so she was able to go to the game with us in the freezing rain. There we were, Glenn, Lacie, Jonathan, and myself, sitting on ice-cold aluminum bleachers in green slickers under a blanket watching Logan play football. We couldn't see the field for the rain, and we couldn't stop laughing at each other. We were determined to

enjoy our nachos and Cokes, even if they were both mixed with rain water. It was a cold, wet, and wonderful day—the kind of day you
cherish for the rest of your life—the kind of day that is easy to let slip by until you realize you'll never get another one like it.

I wanted a perfect family, and that is just what I got. I would stare at our family pictures and think, *This is what I have been waiting for*. Really, I was that shallow. My happiness revolved around how we looked on the outside, in photos, and to the neighbors. I was obsessed with appearances. Don't get me wrong, I wanted our real lives to match the perfect appearance, but I needed that perfect appearance, and so I continued to monitor who Glenn would talk to and spend time with. If he was friendly with people who drank or even looked like they might do drugs, I was on guard and trying to run interference. Any influence on him that wasn't good in my view—from church or an FFA parent or a coach—I saw as threats to our perfect, little world. - were treated as threats. They might influence him to resort back to the old him. He had vowed not to be the old him so that he could have a new life with me and my boys, and I knew that he meant it. I watched him day in and day out work to keep his vow, but for some reason it was never enough. Even with the vow and good intentions, I could see him struggle sometimes. He worked in the oilfield with a lot of guys who drank and used.

Glenn was always kind to everyone, and it terrified me that he would slip up. I knew from him that he and a drinking and drug problem, and learned from his mom the way he had changed during the war.

"He just wasn't the same person that left," she told me. Glenn snuck off to the army to begin with, which his parents weren't thrilled about.

"We were afraid he'd get killed over there," his mom said. "I never even imagined it'd do what it did to him."

She went on to tell me how when Glenn came back he was in constant trouble. His father, who Glenn adored, was always there to bail him out of jail. He had endless patience with his prodigal son. I didn't want to have to exercise the same kind of patience or see that man return, and so I was vigilant about who Glenn was around. So when he befriended a younger guy from the oilfield that I knew had a rough reputation, I badgered him about it every time the kid dropped by. The kid would come over and Glenn would go out and smoke cigarettes with him. I'd peek through the window at the two of them. Every time they were doing the same thing: leaning back on the bed of Glenn's truck, talking and kicking rocks. I didn't get why the kid had to come to Glenn.

"What do you need to go outside with Curtis, Glenn? I just don't like the influence he could have. We have plenty of friends from church. You don't need to spend time with Curtis."

"The point is the influence I have on him, Kim," Glenn

would tell me.

"It isn't worth it," I'd huff. "I don't like that you smoke cigarettes when he is around. What would our pastor think if he saw you?"

"He'd think I was giving a young man who needs it advice, I hope."

"Our life is perfect, Glenn. I just don't know why you have to have people like that around," I'd protest.

"You need to take off those rose-colored glasses," Glenn would say when I got to caught up in how perfect our life was. "What people think about us doesn't matter. And everything isn't always pure and good."

"What's that supposed to mean?" I'd ask.

"Sometimes things just suck, and those are facts," he'd tell me really matter-of-factly. "And sometimes your friendship is needed outside your little circle of friends."

"That's ridiculous," I'd scoff, rolling my eyes. We had a perfect life, and I saw no harm in making sure it stayed that way.

XXXXX

5

When the Past Comes a-Callin'

AS time passed, I found myself worrying more and more about Glenn's past. We had spent years laughing at his stories, but I found myself feeling more and more uneasy when he'd tell a story about him and the guys in Germany. The stories morphed from amusing anecdotes to something a little more sinister. Before, I could leave the past in the past and laugh off the crazy days Glenn had experienced, but the past started to move into the present for me. It was weird, because it had never bothered me before, but I had this sinking feeling that it wasn't completely gone. When it finally hit me that

I had a relentless mass of anxiety plaguing me about Glenn, I realized that in reality, it had been there all along. It was the reason I called constantly when he was with certain people and got irritated when he spent evenings in the driveway with men with what I considered loose morals. I had always known that drinking and drugs were a part of Glenn's life when he was stationed overseas. What I had been blind to was the fact that I was haunted by it.

"Did I tell you about the time me and a bunch of the guys rented a limo to go see Styx in concert? It cost us an arm and a leg, but it was worth it because we knew we could drink the place dry and have a ride home," he told me one time, laughing a little about how ridiculous his life used to be. I had laughed at so many of those stories, until they quit being funny. I didn't know how to tell Glenn though. I didn't know how to say, "I'm terrified sometimes about what kind of consequences we'll face because of your past." I also couldn't stand the fact that no matter how much I could control my present, there was absolutely nothing I could do about what was behind us.

Glenn told his old war stories so much, my boys knew them by heart. Even when Glenn wasn't there to tell them, whenever an old Aerosmith or Doobie Brothers song would come on the radio, one of my son's would launch into his practiced and perfected Glenn impression.

"It was 1972; we were at Stuttgart Germany when they put on a crazy concert. It was a rough night," Logan would say, his voice lowered and his arms going just like Glenn's when he would tell a story. He would lean back in a chair and pretend to smoke a cigarette as he took on Glenn's character. I would laugh, but seeing my son pretend to smoke a cigarette and talk about getting blacked out drunk settled wrong with me.

"You're so funny," Glenn would tease.

Even as we made a running joke of it, I worried endlessly that demons he gained during those years in Germany would surface in my world. Glenn laughed off those days, but I knew there was more beneath the surface. Every time he told a story, his mother's words echoed in my ear: "He just wasn't the same person that left." Glenn was no longer the drunken druggie he was during Vietnam, but something in him had changed; his own mother had admitted that. I feared what I could not know—when that person he was during the war might return.

Glenn was eighteen when he enlisted in the Army; in other words, he was young and impressionable. It was the early seventies when he went into the Army and the culture was nothing like it is now. Glenn always told us about the "anything goes" mentality that he and all the soldiers lived by. The Army was less about discipline and more about getting away with what you could. You can imagine what that looked like for a bunch of eighteen-year-olds fresh out of high school, on their own for the first time. It meant that everyone took everything too far. Glenn made that clear through all his stories.

I never knew if Glenn thought about his past the same way I did. I assumed he didn't. Where I saw the threat of addiction returning or health consequences, I imagined he saw only great dinner conversation and a way to entertain friends when they were over for game night. I don't know if it had anything to do with his own concerns about the abuse he had put his body through, but in 2008 he decided to take advantage of his VA benefits and scheduled a complete physical. A true Texas cowboy and a stereotypical man, Glenn was not the kind to run to the doctor for a runny nose or an achy joint. He went to the doctor only when he had to or I forced him to, which was rare because he was a healthy man for the most part. That is why I was a little surprised when he mentioned scheduling a physical. I was also happy to hear it. Maybe, I thought, I could put some of my fears to rest once a doctor looked him over—not all of them, mind you, but some.

Whatever prompted Glenn to get checked out, I don't think he was expecting any big news to come out of it. He just figured it was free and he was older, so he may as well go in and get everything checked out.

"Wouldn't hurt to get my cholesterol checked I suppose," he said when I asked what made him decide to go.

"Not that I'm complaining," I was sure to add.

The relief I felt upon hearing Glenn was getting a physical was soon eclipsed by the fear that rather than getting rid of my fear, the check-up might actually confirm them. Once again, I was not in control. Not only that, the physical hadn't even happened, so I had to wait to find out if I had wasted my worry or not. And so I turned to God, as I did when I was feeling out of control. I prayed about it every night.

"God, I just need Glenn to be healthy, and things will be fine. Just make Glenn okay. His heathen ways are behind him now, so let this go well so we can leave it all behind us."

My prayers comforted me. I told God what I needed, and I waited.

"Well? What did the doctor say?" I asked when I knew Glenn had gotten the results. I had prayed, so I waited for confirmation God was listening.

"It's all pretty good," he told me. I knew him well. There was more.

"So what all did he say?"

"I don't want you to get all worked up, but there was a little bad news. I have some liver damage from my time overseas."

My heart sank. I knew it. I just knew it! I knew that his past was going to come back. Before I could say anything,

Glenn went on, "The doctor told me he was not alarmed at all with the amount of damage, so this really isn't a big deal, baby."

"You can't drink at all anymore," I stated. I didn't suggest; I stated.

"I'm fine with that, but I want to tell you that he told me he sees this all the time in men who served in Vietnam. There's a ton of men out there with the same problem, living their lives and doing fine. They do want to do treatments though."

I was skeptical. If the doctor was so unconcerned, I didn't see why he would feel it necessary to start treatment on his liver. I tried not to scold. Glenn knew what had caused this, so I didn't need to remind him. I would, however, be sure that alcohol never touched his lips again.

The treatments were expensive, and if we wanted the government to cover them we had to get Glenn to Shreveport, Louisiana, where the closet VA was to us. For weeks, we travelled back and forth from Texas to Louisiana, first to figure out what the plan of attack would be, and then to start the treatments. After weeks of visits, they came up with a treatment plan and some serious changes that Glenn would have to make. The rules from the doctor, as far as lifestyle changes, were pretty straightforward and to the point—no drinking ever again. When the doctor told us this, I saw it as an opportunity rather than a restriction. Now it wasn't just me telling him not to drink; it was the doctor. I could rest and let the doctor play the role of bad guy now. I had wanted him to stop altogether for some time, just because I thought it would play a positive role in our lives and our faith. Glenn had never showed any signs of a problem once we were married, but I always worried about his addictive personality. Drinking also didn't fit into the image I had of our perfect life.

It took about eighteen months of taking pills every day (something like chemotherapy treatments) and monthly shots for blood conditioning to get his liver enzyme number count back to normal. During the eighteen months of treatment, we also talked with a counselor monthly. This was eye-opening for me. Up to that point, I had never considered his past as traumatic or understood the kind of impact his time over there had on him. He always told his stories like they were scenes from a comedy, an off-colored, PG-13 comedy, but a comedy none the less. The more conversations we had sitting in that counselor's office, the more I began to realize that there was much more to the time he spent overseas serving his country.

I sat quietly next to my husband as he talked about parts of his life I never knew existed. He had always been so open; I assumed I knew everything, but there was so much more. Often, we would continue the conversations on the car ride home. Other times Glenn wanted to let them stay there in that office. He didn't want them leaving the room with us. The fact of the matter was, they couldn't stay there.

I found out that, all stories of wild nights and rock concerts aside, Glenn had a tough time during his years of enlistment. He missed his family terribly and being away from them forded Glenn to come to terms with some things he hadn't before he'd shipped off to serve overseas. He talked about long letters he had written his dad apologizing for always being a problem child as he was growing up. He had two brothers and a sister, and he was the only one that was constantly causing his folks heartaches. He began to regret that as he matured. Unfortunately, he was half a world away from the people he felt he needed to make amends with. That weighed heavy on his heart and conscience.

As I listened to Glenn open up, I began to see that he was as insecure as I was about being accepted by others. His insecurity started with a fear of rejection by his own family, who he thought he'd caused so much trouble for.

The pain of being away from his family was just the tip of the iceberg. As we delved deeper into his past, I realized how detrimental the war had been to all those who were a part of it. To hear Glenn explain it, it sounded as if the war had completely changed the men, physically and mentally. The stress and the trauma they encountered were unsettling. He always told me that he was never involved in actual conflict since he processed soldiers who were returning from the battlefield. I thought that since he never had to fire a gun at another person, he must have avoided all the scars that war leaves. I was wrong.

I found out that even if Glenn wasn't face-to-face with the enemy, the stories the men he worked with told and the damage he saw that had been done to their bodies, in his words, was haunting. I saw a side of Glenn that was vulnerable in a way I could have never imagined. He wasn't an invincible man capable of anything and scared of nothing. He was just a boy who missed his mom and dad and wanted nothing more than to be home.

Drinking and doing drugs became Glenn's way to cope with his homesickness and his fear until he could get back home and make things right again. He ended up getting in quite a bit of trouble during his tours. He never did anything big—just an onslaught of dumb, young kid stuff that added up over time. I always thought his little run-ins were the product of a hardheaded, immature kid who didn't want to be told what to do. I discovered that his little episodes were a tactic to get back home to the States. He figured if he acted out enough, they wouldn't want him anymore, and he could leave that hellhole. All of this was news to me.

I watched as this adult—this handsome, charismatic cowboy—opened up to me and to the therapist. It was strange how the power dynamic shifted. When we first walked in and sat down to introduce ourselves, I thought there was no way Glenn was going to give the therapist what she wanted. He was tough and independent; he didn't need a shrink to straighten him out. He had real-life know-how, and she had a laundry list of degrees, which we saw proof of hanging on the office walls. In that office with all those degrees, Glenn became a boy with low self-esteem who just wanted to be noticed. He talked with her with great detail. I would place my hand on his knee or touch his leg gently to tell him—I am here for you—keep talking. I felt like I was the strong one at those times. He was huge and I was small in comparrison, but he was leaning on me. That explained so much about his personality. It also explained his relationship with his parents.

I always admired how much he loved his parents. I thought it was so thoughtful the way we made the five-hour journey to Sweetwater as often as possible just to visit them. He and his dad were so close. When his dad passed, he was devastated. I knew how close the two were, but understanding their past helped me better understand Glenn and his dedication to them.

Every time we walked out of the office, I would pray that I would be able to handle the things I was learning about my husband the way I was supposed to. At first, I didn't know how probing into his most vulnerable places would affect me or our marriage. I realized, though, it just made me love him more.

"You should know," the doctor warned me after one of our sessions, "that during this treatment he may become irritable and hard to manage. He will have good days and bad days, but the bad days may become more than you can handle by yourself."

"How bad are you thinking?" I asked.

"I'm not saying it will happen, but he may get violent," she told me. *Violent*? I thought. Could Glenn actually become a threat to me and the kids? I couldn't even imagine it.

"Here's my number in case anything should happen. If you ever feel like things are getting out of hand, you call me, and I will deal with him directly. And, Kim, if this does happen, I want you to leave the house immediately with the kids and call. I am serious. Do not try to calm him down. Just leave and let me deal with it. That's my job, okay?"

"Okay," I replied. My head was spinning at the very thought of my husband becoming so out of control I'd have to flee my own home. I took the number, though, and thanked her. She placed her number in my hand then held it tightly for an extended few seconds.

Having children in the house made it crucial for us to maintain a normal household, so I was willing to do whatever it took to keep things as normal as possible. Once or twice we did get a little out of sorts, but corrections were made, and we got back on track with little hurt feelings. Violence never became a factor, thank God.

Glenn stuck to the game plan after the initial treatments. There was no more drinking, and he tried to be better to his body. But in his follow-up appointments, we found out that the liver enzymes were slowly returning to the same that they had been before the treatment, which meant that his liver was not functioning properly again. I remember standing in the room hearing the doctor give us the sombering news. I hated the VA it was so sad there and I just wanted to leave the room and drive quickly home. That was not easy to hear after having watched him spend a year and a half on a strict regimen of ribavirin and nuepregene, which was not exactly easy on a person. It was eighteen months of nausea and sleepless nights. When the test results came back bad again, they told us that our best option was to start the process all over again. I couldn't imagine another eighteen months of that for Glenn. I knew it had been hell for him. I felt the rug pulled from under me once again. Glenn explained to everyone that he would not go through treatment again.

Why God? I asked. *We have done everything we need to. Why?*

At about the same time we got the bad news about Glenn's health, his boss told him about a cowboy church in the area he and his wife had been attending.

"I'll try to check it out some time," Glenn told his boss every time he mentioned it, just to be cordial, but we never made it. Sunday morning would always roll around, and there'd be something that had to be done, or we just felt too tired and beat down to get around and go. We were comfortable in our routine, so we never made it to the church. Then one Sunday morning Glenn woke up early and said, "Get dressed; we are going to the cowboy church."

It had been quite some time since we had attended church at that point. I always prayed and considered myself a person of faith, but there was his crazy work schedule and the countless months of health problems. When Glenn announced that we were going to try out the church, I didn't ask questions. I hopped out of bed and got going! We may have been out of church, but it was like something inside me said, "Kim, this is what your life has been missing. Get up and go!"

I had never been to a cowboy church, so I had no idea what kind of attire it called for. I put on a leather skirt and jacket with a pair of boots. I went all out in what I imagined must be the cowboy version of Sunday's best.

"I should have told you," Glenn said when he saw me emerge from the bedroom dressed to the hilt. "They meet in a tent."

"What?" I asked.

"It's a new church," he explained. "They own land but haven't built anything on it yet. We need to wear warm jeans and bring blankets and lawn chairs."

"Okay," I said, thrown off guard. "I'll go change."

As I slipped into a pair of jeans and started gathering blankets, all I could think was, *what in the world are we going to?* I had never in my life heard of having church in a tent. let alone bringing lawn chairs and blankets along. It felt like we were going to a ball game, not a church service. The excitement I had earlier that morning about getting involved in a church began to fade as I pictured myself in a lawn chair out in the middle of some field. I tried to keep my enthusiasm about it though. If Glenn was willing to go to church, I was happy to escort him.

"Dan told me about another guy who goes to this church who has a liver disease, too," Glenn said to me on the way to the service. Dan was another man he worked with at the time. "They've been praying for him, and the guy's been making some progress."

I smiled and said that was great, but thought the whole thing sounded a little weak. I tried to push back my skepticism and give this a shot. We were, after all, searching for any kind of answers.

To get to the tent where the cowboy church would be held, we drive through a massive pasture. Along the way we passed two porta-potties. That was the first time I'd passed a porta-potty on my way to my seat in church. On the top of a hill there was a giant tent- the kind they hold circuses in. Outside the tent were rows of parked trucks with a few cars in the mix. There were also horses waiting in trailers for an after-church ride. As skeptical as I had been that morning, the second my foot touched that pasture grass, I was a believer. The moment I opened the truck door, I felt like I was on holy ground. The presence of the Lord was so strong. It turns out you don't need bricks to build a house of worship after all.

"All we are doing here today is meeting this man, David. I just want to get some information from him about the doctor he sees, and we are out of here," Glenn said as we headed for the tent. "This is just an information-gathering trip. I'd rather talk to someone who's been through it than try to pick someone from the yellow pages I know nothing about."

I nodded in response. I knew that we needed to find something better than the VA doctor. We both realized fairly soon that the VA wasn't the best choice. With a condition like Glenn's, we needed someone who specialized in liver disease. We hoped the man at the church could give us some names of specialists to get better treatment.

During the service that day, every time the wind blew, the sides of the big top would slap so hard against themselves that you could hardly hear what the preacher was saying. The floor was sawdust over sheets of plywood it was dusty as folks moved around the interior of the "Big Top." Even with the constant interruptions, I felt something special happening in that tent. The preaching was great, and the music was awesome. Everyone there was so relaxed and friendly. I knew we were there to get information about a doctor, but I was so glad that we had come. I knew that something bigger was happening.

After the service, we found the man Dan had told us about. We stopped and talked to him and his wife for a bit about his liver problems. Sure enough, his liver had stopped deteriorating under the care and treatment of his new doctor. He looked thin and it was obvious he had been very sick but he was there worshipping the Lord.. This was good news—the reason we came to the church. Glenn got his doctor's name to schedule an appointment with him. We got what we came for and left. The very next morning Glenn called and scheduled an appointment. He went to the see the specialist that same week.

The new doctor ran all the tests and found that the enzyme count was just as the VA said it was.

"We can sustain this elevated count just as long as it stops rising," the doctor told us. "There will come a point that you will need to do a transplant, but that is in the future. The bad news is that since the count rose so quickly after treatment, the outcome will probably not be as good as we would like."

We had a lot to think about after the appointment. We knew by what the doctor said it wouldn't be long before Glenn would be on a transplant list. Things weren't going as I had hoped at all.

In the midst of the bad news, I suggested we go tc the cowboy church again and give it another try. Something kept pulling at me, telling me I needed to go back. Glenn agreed, so went for a second time. This time I didn't put on a skirt. I got right into my warm clothes and gathered the blankets. I also made sure to use the little girl's room before I left. Those porta-potties looked frightening.

We made the journey back to that strangely hallowed ground. That day the man who had the liver disease asked the church if they could do for Glenn what they had done for him.

"If you don't mind, I'd like to call you up front and pray for healing," he said

Everyone there seemed excited about the idea. Glenn, however, was not thrilled about getting in front of people, even if it was for healing. He ultimately agreed, and we all gathered around, laid hands on him, and prayed. It was amazing all these large cowboy type men gathering around. Some had on spurs clicking and clanging up front to the alter before joining hands and hearts around us. So powerful. Completely unchartered territory for me/us.

The drive home was surreal; no words were spoken. I think we were both a little taken aback by the love and concern these folks expressed. As reluctant as Glenn was about going up to the front of the church that day, I think he realized that something special had happened that day. We didn't know what exactly, but something otherworldly had touched both of us.

The next week Glenn had the regular monthly doctor visit to draw some blood and monitor liver enzymes. The results showed a much lower liver enzyme count. It wasn't just lower; the count was low enough that he was almost in normal range. The doctor and nurse came into the room together to tell us.

"We have some good news," the doctor said, "Really good news. There is no explanation for this, but your enzyme count is almost normal." He went on to say how this just could not be possible.

Glenn chuckled and said, "I know exactly what happened."

That day when we left the doctor's office, the sky was bluer and the grass was greener. I felt like I had woken up from a bad dream. Life was good—no, it was great!

Glenn went back to church the next Sunday, got up in front of the church, and told his story, which alone was a miracle. He grabbed the microphone and talked about God's amazing grace. I felt like I was looking at another man standing up there. He almost looked like he was at ease being in front of the crowd. Standing up in front of an entire congregation, he went over all the details of the visit he had with the doctor. He thanked everyone for praying over him, and he thanked me for hanging in there with him. I was so proud of him. Finally, life was as it should be.

So—How did we get here?

XXXXX

6

How Did We Get Here?

JULIE and I stood beside one another in corridor wondering where to go. The nurse, too focused on the task at hand to think about me in the midst of all the chaos, failed to tell me what I was supposed to do before the doors shut. She just swooped in, said Glenn needed to move, put him in an elevator, asked him if he had a DNR, and then they were gone. Because I didn't see Glenn anywhere, I assumed he was already in his room. There was no way, I thought, we could have beaten the elevator down. But then the elevator doors began to open—the elevator that Glenn was on—the elevator

I heard that nurse say those words that were still ringing hard in my ears: "We need to know, do you want to be resuscitated if you code in this elevator? Do you have a directive on file?" I felt the life slip out of my body when I thought about those words and realized Glenn was still on that elevator. Something horrible must have happened. My breath caught in my throat.

Two nurses popped out of the elevator and apologized for the delay.

"We had to go back for a replacement machine," one of the nurses said quickly as she passed me.

My heart thudded hard under my ribs—so hard it seemed to make my body quiver with every beat. I felt it in my fingertips and at the back of my skull. I heard it in my ears. I didn't know if it was from running down the stairs or the intensity of the situation. All of my senses seemed to cross paths so that I couldn't make sense of much. I finally sucked in a gulp of air and took off after the nurses—after Glenn.

I tried not to let my mind wonder as I trailed the rolling bed that carried my husband. I had no idea what I would see when we all finally stopped. How do you prepare for something like that? How do you make sense of something that is so random and unfair that there is no sense to find? I just wanted to take my husband and go home. I wanted to say, "enough!" and be done with hospitals and nurses and giant metal contraptions that made terrible noises.

"This way," the nurse called back to me as they wheeled Glenn down another hallway. They rushed us into a large room. Sunlight poured in from an enormous window with open blinds, bathing all of us in a faint, yellow glow. I looked out the window for a moment. I could see daylight and people outside in the courtyard, chatting and sipping coffee. I wondered, *Do they have any idea what is going on in here?*

I quit looking at the strangers outside, lost in their own little worlds, and I turned to Glenn. He was alive, and he looked fine. There was nothing startling—no glazed eyes or death pale complexion. It was just Glenn. Relief washed over me, but then as our eyes meet, I saw fear and confusion in his. The panic that had waned waxed again. A hard knot clogged my throat. I wanted to cry, but instead I was strong, as always. I swallowed my fear and smiled at him.

"You look great. What took you so long?" I asked, putting a hand on his.

I convinced myself as I stood there by Glenn's side that this was just a small setback. People were rushing around the bed, getting monitors set up, taking Glenn's blood pressure, and calling out numbers. I saw his expression soften as everything buzzed around us. My strength helped him, even if it was just an act. That was enough for me. In fact, I had also convinced myself that things were okay.

"This is the best floor in the hospital," the nurses assured him with friendly smiles on their faces. "You are in good hands."

The young, dark-haired head nurse who had made the shattering announcement about coding in the elevator began to explain to me that her assistant, who was replacing a fluid bag as we spoke, was the best of the best. I nodded and looked over at the nurse she was talking about. Her long hair was pulled back into a neat ponytail. She was thin, almost too thin. She seemed to lack any personality whatsoever. I studied her as she worked like a robot, never speaking, her expression unchanging.

"She will be with you all day, and you are in good hands," the head nurse repeated.

The mechanical nurse didn't look up even once as her boss sang her praises. As I watched her, I saw something in her movements. In her blank expression, I caught the quickest hint at emotion. She was distressed, overworked on a critical care unit floor. She was moving quickly and efficiently to get through what she needed to so she could move on to the next patient that needed her. She was hurried, but deliberate to the point that it looked like she was born to do what she was doing. I realized that the moment she had Glenn set up, she would rush into the next room, and then the next, and the next, and have to work with the same sense of urgency. I thought about terrible the job must be, working with extremely ill patients hour after hour, day after day.

"I am pleased to meet you," Glenn said in an attempt to connect with robotic nurse. "Have you worked here at the hospital for a long time?"

Glenn's voice was soft and kind. He spoke to all the nurses that way. He was constantly apologizing to his nurses for being too much trouble. I never spoke when they would come into to check vitals or administer medication, but Glenn was always friendly, always trying to make others feel appreciated, even as he battled flesh-eating bacteria that was ravishing his midsection. Through it all, he remained cordial and warm to whomever walked into his room.

"I have worked here for seven years and have lived in Gladewater for many years," the nurse answered, blunt and to the point. She answered the way I imagined a new Army recruit answers a drill sergeant. There is no small talk; she said enough to answer the questions she was asked, and she was back to work.

I put down the bags, clothes, and flowers I had been juggling floor to floor. Julie found a clear place on a boxed windowsill to put all the things she had been holding down. Afterwards, she wrapped her arms around me, squeezed me tightly, and whispered, "It will be all right," in my ear as she held me. When she finally let me go, she left to call our church to give them an update on Glenn. Not even a minute after Julie was gone, the head nurse came back in.

"I think you should probably start calling family," she told me. "Get everyone here."

Why? I wanted to ask, but instead I just started dialing numbers. Glenn and I had been in the hospital for weeks, and we still knew hardly anything about the disease that was keeping him sick. I had gotten used to not knowing. I didn't like it, but I was used to it.

When Lacie, Glenn's daughter, answered the phone, I realized I had no idea what to tell her, or my boys for that fact. I couldn't answer any questions about anything. All I could say was, "Glenn's hit another hurdle, so we need everyone to come up."

I went through the list of relatives—my kids, his brother and sister, who lived five hours away. Even as I called to tell people to get there quick, I still believed we'd be going home any day. In between phone calls, I thought about what I needed to do to fix everything. I thought about how to get Glenn back home so we could get back to the lives we had left—back to the cowboy church we had fallen in love with and to our bible studies.

Julie called the church for me as I spoke to relatives. Soon after I talked to his siblings, one of Glenn's nieces went crazy calling the hospital room and nurse's station demanding answers. I had told her just to get there, and fast. It was all I knew at the time—all the doctor had told me. That wasn't enough for her though. It wasn't enough for me either, but it was all we had. Soon my cell started ringing, and then Glenn's. It was his niece. I never answered. What was I going to say, anyway? I had more important matters—Glenn. As much as I wanted to believe we were going home, there was something inside me that knew this would be our final moments together, and I wasn't going to miss a second. At some point, the nurse came in and ripped the phone cord out of the wall.

With the phone no longer ringing, I sat quietly and I began to talk to God.

I don't know what today holds, and we really need you. Oh, Lord, we are praying and waiting on you to see us through this. We are trusting that today will end with renewed strength. We just need you to get us home right now—get us out of this.

The doctor came in as I was praying. We had come to know him well. I could tell when he was coming down the hallway just by cadence of his footsteps. When he entered the room, he didn't go through his usual routine. He didn't read Glenn's chart or ask how we were feeling. He just started talking.

"If something doesn't change, you are going to die today," he said. His candor startled me. I thought for a moment he was playing some cruel joke, but he never smiled.

"Since you are alert and coherent, I need to know what you feel about life support? Do you want to be revived in the event you stop breathing? We need to make sure we know these things while you are able to answer."

I felt the world stop spinning. He may as well have plunged a knife in my heart. The doctor had been so wonderful to us since Glenn first came in with pain in his side, but suddenly his words seemed so harsh and cold. I blinked hard looking at him, and began to think that maybe I had misunderstood him. There was no way, I thought, that he was talking to us, like *that. There must be a mistake,* I told myself. *Death is not an option. Glenn dying is not how this ends.*

I knew that the doctor had to be wrong. I had been praying too hard for him to be right. Leaving without Glenn was not the plan. I would not accept it.

"Your body is shutting down, and what you are feeling right now is the results of that effect," the doctor continued. "Your kidneys and liver are not functioning well and you cannot sustain unless those organs get back in line."

I had noticed Glenn's shortness of breath—the way he was breathing in short, shallow motions. But that wasn't anything new. When that happened, we would just get a cold compress, and Glenn would say, "Kim, breathe with me, help me slow my breath down."

I would breathe slowly and rhythmically, my hand on Glenn's chest as I did, and he would eventually slow his breath down to match mine. I thought it was happening because he was nervous or when the pain got to be overwhelming. I told myself, *He will be fine as soon as he calms down. It has been a busy couple of hours*. What I didn't realize was that the trouble breathing was a warning sign to us of something that had gone awry inside of Glenn. It was much worse than a case of nerves or a reaction to pain.

"After getting to know you in the last thirty days, I know that you are a Christian, so I feel confident talking with you about this," the doctor said. His words were clear and sharp, but they were also compassionate and kind. "Look, I'm asking you to make some very tough decisions right now, but I am certain of my choice to speak directly to you about today's outcome. I don't need to ask anyone else in your family; I feel you are more than capable to make your own decision. So, do you want to be revived and put on life support if you stop breathing today?" the doctor asked again. He was looking only at Glenn when he asked.

The room suddenly shrunk around me as the doctor asked that question. Everything began to feel like it was closing in one me—the walls, the hospital, the world. I was not prepared in the least to hear something like that. Even if I had been aware how bad Glenn had gotten, I don't think I could have handled those words.

In less time than it took to watch a sitcom, we had gone from hoping Glenn would be released soon to have two options, both of which were terrible. No matter what, they both meant our lives would forever changed, and not in a good way. My fairy tale was coming to an end. My legs trembled as I listened to the doctor go on.

"Glenn, listen to me; it is your choice, and this is something most people do not get to decide for themselves because they are not coherent enough to make a decision. I want you to know everything. Life support will only delay the end for a short time. Your kidneys and liver are not functioning correctly, and nothing can be done about that."

The doctor was so confident about what he said—so certain about Glenn's death. I couldn't stand it. He was just "business as usual" about it. He didn't even entertain the idea that Glenn would recover—didn't even mention what a miracle could do. He had implied he was a Christian. How could he think that the end was so inevitable? I was indignant that a man who believed in God could believe that there was no way out of our situation. Even as he more or less read him his last rites, I still believed that his illness was yet another crisis that we would be victorious over, just like his liver problem had been. I just had to pray, and promise God we would never forget the very hard times. If I did that, I was sure God would rescue us.

God, I am scared, I started to pray, and as I was working to explain to God what He needed to do for us immediately, I heard Glenn's wonderful voice.

"I understand, Doc, and I do not want to be resuscitated if I die today."

Who was this person talking? Why, I wanted to know, would Glenn not want to do everything to stay alive. Anyone in their right mind would choose life over death! What was he doing? Why was he saying he wanted to die that day?

"God's will is what will go on here today, and I just have to trust we will get through this," Glenn said.

No! No! I thought. *God's will is that Glenn survives. It has to be! I have prayed for it day and night.*

"Okay then," the doctor replied, and I swore I saw a victorious smile sneak onto his face. "We will need to go over everything with the nurses."

At that, he turned to me and asked, "Can you step into the hall with me for just a moment, Mrs. Hicks?" I nodded quiet when all I wanted to do was scream. "Glenn, I will be back shortly to check on you," he said before he ushered me into the hall. The last thing I wanted to do was leave Glenn's side, but I could see the doctor needed to say something to me. Reluctantly I followed him out into the hall. My muscles twitched beneath my skin. I want so badly to be by Glenn's side in that moment.

"He may be able to fight this off, but I don't have much hope that will happen," he told me. I went numb. I had no idea what I was supposed to say to that, so I said nothing at all. The doctor must have noticed that he was overwhelming me. He stopped his death sentence talk to ask if I was okay. I nodded out of habit. *Sure, I am fine. Why wouldn't I be?*

He went on, speaking very directly to me the way someone speaks when they have said the same thing again and again.

"As the day progresses, you might want to change the resuscitate orders. As friends and family come in, they may encourage you to, but I would remind them of his decision," he lectured, almost in an admonishing tone. Again, I said nothing. I just blinked. I blinked and I thought, *Okay, God, any minute now.*

"Someone will be by to get your signature," he said finally. And with that, he was gone—on to the next patient.

That evening, when his shift was over, he would go home to his family while I was still there in that hospital, figuring out a way to piece my family back together. What a difference a day can make.

I didn't know what to do with the information that was dumped in my lap and in my life. Who would? All I knew was that I had to get back into the room. If I missed one second with Glenn, it will truly be a moment that I would never get back. No time to think, no time to breathe. I wiped the tears back and pushed the door open.

"What did he say to you out there?" Glenn asked.

"He said we are gonna lick this thing! I told him how strong you are and that there is no way are we giving up."

Something inside of me was so proud of the man lying in that bed.

"I am okay," he said to me. Those blue eyes were still bright and wide open. *How is it possible?* I wondered. *How is he so clam and steady?*

I had made the phone calls. I had done everything I had been asked to do. All I could think was, *What next? What do I need to prepare for?* I was still positive, still waiting for my miracle and testimony, but it was becoming clear to me that we were in a dire situation—one I had been dodging and denying from the time we entered the hospital.

XXXXX

7

Letting Go and Letting God, Finally

HE didn't scream and cry that day. He didn't immediately say, "Get a preacher! I better get things straight with God."

"How are you doing, baby?" I asked him over and over. I didn't know what to say anymore. The words "I love you" seemed to be so small and unworthy of my true feelings. They don't make words powerful enough to express what I felt about Glenn in those moments.

"I'm just trusting in God," he said to me every time I asked the question. Even on his deathbed, he wore that charming smile I had fallen in love with. He was so calm, so sure of everything, which I could not wrap my head around. I had never felt so unstable in all my life, and there Glenn was, moving through it all with grace. I was constantly on the verge of unravelling, but then I'd look at him, I'd see the peacefulness that shone in him, and I'd find strength somewhere deep down inside me to keep going. I was borrowing strength from him.

I had spent so much time in the hospital at that point. Evening after evening, I was there, curled up on Glenn's bed watching a movie on a small DVD player I had brought from home. I had to cram myself right next to him just to see the tiny screen. Of course, I complained because we were crowded on the small bed and it was so uncomfortable at times. But being that close to him, I could smell him—not cologne or soap, just *him*. That smell, of his skin and his hair, was as good as the best cologne, maybe better. Even if it was uncomfortable, that was fine because it didn't seem like I could ever get close enough to him, especially in the final hours. As strange as it sounds, hospital rooms had become a kind of couple's retreat for us—one we both needed at the time. Since the time we had fallen in love, so much had happened. Life and silly quarrels over trivial things had built a wedge between us. We had made a commitment to each other, and we would honor it, but the road was tough sometimes. The months before Glenn was admitted to the hospital for what we thought would be a quick in-an-out visit been particularly draining. We were still in it for the long run, but there was no doubt about it, we were in a rut.

Suddenly, I found myself mesmerized by his face, hands, and eyes, like I was when we first met. There were those beautiful blue eyes that I made first contact with in that hotel parking lot in Tyler, Texas, where I made a fool of myself all those years before—my handsome cowboy that became my husband, my love, my best friend. All the shoulda, coulda, wouldas that passed us by came back to me in a swell of emotions and memories. All the times I should have forgiven and forgot but instead held onto my principles and made myself bitter and hateful came roaring back. One by one I remember all the times we argued over silly stuff that made no difference. Glenn's sickness seemed to bring us where we needed to be. It was the worst and best thing that could have happened to us—at first.

Before it came down to making phone calls to the family, we had talked about how we were going to share this journey with anyone and everyone who came into our path. We worked on it every night as we sat and waited for healing to come. We knew—*I* knew—that we had the Lord, and that He would not let us down. I knew that in the scriptures He had promised to hold us and that He was with us through the worst of situations. Sitting there at Glenn's bedside, I was absolutely in my worst situation. But I focused on the fact that God had everything under control, and so we would walk out those hospital doors victoriously. I had it all figured out. All God needed to do was keep His end of the deal and we were set. I thought that we just needed to work during this downtime on focusing on God's will for our lives. Not once in all the praying and believing did it occur to me that God *was* busy working, just not in the direction I assumed or wanted Him to. I may have been listening, but I was only listening for what I wanted to hear. Glenn knew that, but I didn't.

God was saying to me, "Slow down, listen and enjoy this time" all along, but I couldn't hear that because it wasn't what I was listening for. I wanted God to come in and heal Glenn, but the life He was changing was mine. Glenn already had everything under control. He was sure of his fate, and so no matter what happened, he knew he would be fine. Unlike me, he didn't demand a certain outcome to see God working. Glenn saw God already in a way I could not.

Glenn continued to greet everyone who came by with a smile and a story. He would start with, "The Lord painted the portrait of my life before I came to be. I have put people and situations into my portrait that don't belong there, but in God's awesome wisdom, he simply erases them out and put things back right. Every road I ruined is repaired, and I have to believe he has this situation. My portrait was perfected by the Lord, as it was perfect from the start."

He told this story again and again, until he lost consciousness and could no longer tell it anymore. Just before he slipped into a sleep he would never return from, a pastor friend stopped. Of course, Glenn told greeted him with the same story.

"That is truly beautiful, Glenn," the pastor said, his eyes a little red and glassy with tears. "I am blessed beyond words by that awesome testimony."

"This is truly my testimony," Glenn replied with a peaceful smile.

After that, the pastor prayed. When he was done, Glenn asked me to pray with him as well. His words began to sound slurred as we prayed. Some words came out in thick-tongued mumbles, but as sweet as youngsters' prayers at their bedside at night, his words were precious.

Hour after hour he became weaker, but he never lost his peacefulness. There was no fear in his eyes or his words, feeble as they had become. Death, we all knew by that time, was coming, but because of the way Glenn faced it the mood in the room was still somehow positive, even hopeful in a strange way. I could feel the presence of God in the room; it was palpable. It was because of that overwhelming presence that I could still not shake the feeling that everything would be fine. Even with his vitals dropping and the nurses and doctors coming in and reaffirming that it was indeed happening, I couldn't believe it. It seemed too farfetched to think that I would lose my best friend that day—a man who was smiling and praising God for the testimony he had to share with the world.

Even as Glenn began to drift away from us, he was busy doing God's work. I could hear him measuring the church as he slipped in and out—in his mind he was building the church he had worked on until that evening thirty days before we started this tragic journey.

"I love you," I told him as he was fading, and he immediately responded, "I love you too."

All I could do as I watched him wilt like a spring flower was think, *Why can't I fix this? I have always been in charge of everything. God knows that I believe in him, why can't he just get better?* Glenn had his testimony, but I didn't feel I had gotten mine.

We prayed; others prayed. We knew all the right scripture, and I had to believe that things would turn around in a moment. I knew they would. They had to because I *believed* it.

The nurses and doctors were all amazed at the incredible support in our room. They continuously told us what a blessing the day had been for them and what a blessing his life and testimony had been to them. They said as the time came to do a shift change that they would not go home. They just didn't want to leave us. They told me that plenty of medicine had been ordered to make his pain go away, and pain would definitely come in the final hours.

"At the first sign of pain, we would like to begin to inject the solution," the doctor told me. "When we do that, his breathing will also begin to slow down, and that will make the end approach much faster."

The *end*—his life, our life, and our children and friends have come down to *the end*.

"No, we are still waiting on his best friend, our pastor," I told the doctor. "He has to know he has arrived."

Of course, I didn't want him to suffer. I knew he would likely feel some pain eventually, but because our pastor was still on the way, I also wanted him to be as coherent as he could while still being comfortable. I asked the nurses to check him at least every half hour for pain, just to make sure he was still okay. They were more than happy to do this for us, and someone would come in regularly. Each time, a nurse would run an object down his foot or up his leg and then watch him closely for any signs of discomfort. They looked at his face for a change in expression and watched the all the machines that were keeping track of his vitals to see is his heart rate or breathing changed. Once that happened, they would have to administer drugs, which would slow his breathing until his heart finally stopped.

Not once as we waited did he show any sign of pain. The nurses were amazed. Each time, I saw the look of anticipation on their faces. It wasn't that they wanted to give him the medication; years of experience had showed them that pain is what happened at that stage. They had seen this so many times, and they were sure of what would happen. They were certain he would begin to suffer, but he didn't. He never needed pain meds to keep him comfortable. It was like his body knew to hold on—to wait until our pastor had arrived.

"He's probably not going to make it during this life," Terry said. "I hate to say that, I do, but we have to be realistic."

The room was dark and full of people. I had never been so cold or so scared or felt so alone, even as I was surrounded by the people I loved most. I was shaking, at times uncontrollably. I felt like everyone was looking at me—every set of eyes in the room were fixed on me, waiting for me to do something. The kids needed me; I was the person that was supposed fix everything for them, but I couldn't—not this time.

What can I do for them right now? I asked myself as I looked into their teary eyes. And then it finally hit me, *Okay, I can't fix it.*

"Please don't leave me, Glenn," I cried softly into Glenn's ear when it became clear I had no control. "Please hold on! Get better, I know you can. Come on, please." Panicked, I whispered those words over and over into Glenn's ear so no one but him could hear me. Everything inside of me burned with hope and fear and love and sadness. I wanted them to come true so badly that the words exploded from me, even as they were quiet enough only Glenn could hear. Hour after hour I watched and waited for the words to make something happen. I had never wanted anything so badly in all my life. If desperation could bring actions into being, my words would have changes everything that day.

"Please, honey, come back to me," I repeated as his breathing became more and more shallow.

"Hi, Mom," was all that was audible from under his oxygen mask. They had graduated him to one of the masks that covered all of his nose and mouth by that time, so his words were muffled by the heavy plastic. He had been fighting the mask from the moment they put it on him. Several times, he reached to yank it off. Every time, I lowered his hands and tried to soothe him. I couldn't help but remember the doctor's warning that he may get violent at the end. I held my breath each time I calmed him down, hoping that our final moments wouldn't be awful. As he spoke to his mother, he quit fighting; instead, he wore a big smile as he greeted her. She had passed years before. When it hit me that he was talking to his late mother, panic swelled within me. I didn't know if he was hallucinating or truly greeting her. I was losing him, I knew it. He never got agitated though. My touch seemed to put him at ease. I was glad for that, but still my heart ached knowing what was ahead.

To keep myself from dropping to the floor in tears, I focused on his beautiful face and that beautiful smile. All the complaining about the long hours at the hospital, all the words I spoke out of frustration for having to hand him everything, all the times I grumbled as I carried his wound vacuum around the hospital as we walked laps around the halls so Glenn would get better, and the rushing to and from work to make all the doctor meetings; all the days and nights of worry and distress came down to this. I regretted every second of complaint.

Holding on to him for the last time, memorizing his face, examining his hands and combing my hands through his hair, I focused on every detail so the images would be burned into my mind. I never wanted to forget anything about him—the feel of his fingertips on my skin, his salt-and-pepper hair, grayer than it had been years before, the sound of his breath when he exhaled. So handsome was that man. I knew he could feel me holding on to him. He couldn't answer, but I was certain he knew I would not let him go.

As I stroked his neck and head, he leaned into my hand. His eyes were closed, and he was wearing a full oxygen mask so his face was covered, but he still needed my touch. It was a beautiful, peaceful, fleeting moment of life.

I finally spoke quietly into his ear, "Pat will be here in a moment. I love you, and it is okay to leave here and be with Jesus. I will take care of everything."

He needed me to let him go, and as much as I wanted to keep begging him, I knew I had to. I had to say goodbye. I had to give him to God.

I kissed his cheek for the hundredth time that day. That last time he didn't lean into my hand when I stroked his hair. He was leaving me.

Everyone was gathered in the room around the bed. We all watched his chest expand and contract with his slow, easy breaths that became slower and slower. Unlabored and extremely peaceful, he drew breath; something we do all day long without a second thought became a monumental moment each time the cycle was complete. I found myself breathing with him, pacing my breaths with his. It would be the last thing we would do together.

When Pat finally arrived, we all moved down a bit to make room for him. Glenn's best friend had arrived. Everyone was there.

"Okay, buddy, I am here," Pat said as he moved right beside Glenn and scooped his hand up. I watched Pat squeeze Glenn's hand.

"Whoa!" Pat said. "He just squeezed my hand so hard it almost hurt!" A tear sat in the corner of Pat's eye.

We all just broke down and cried at that moment. We knew it was time.

Through it all, Glenn never got a shot for pain. The nurses and doctors had assured us pain was inevitable, but Glenn never winced or whined. There wasn't a single moment he wasn't smiling. That beautiful face of his was peaceful and unstrained through it all.

He breathed his last breaths slower and slower until he finally stopped. *Peaceful* is the only word to describe him.

The nurse stood up slowly and went into action. The first thing she did was turn off the alarm on the heart rate machine. Although the volume was very low, it was still heart-wrenching. Nurse Terry came from a dark corner of the room and checked his pulse and eye dilation. It was over. She unhooked the oxygen machine, exposing his lovely and content face once again. A dear friend began singing "Precious Lord."

Precious Lord, take my hand
lead me on
let me stand,
I am weak
I am tired and I am worn,
through the dawn and through the night
lead on me into the light
Precious Lord.

And then she went straight to "Amazing Grace."

"Amazing grace, how sweet the sound. That saved a wretch like me."

It sounded like an angel was in the room. It was a such beautiful moment. Time stopped as I held onto him, releasing him only to the angels to carry him to heaven. In that moment, I realized that holding Glenn as he passed would be the closest to heaven I would ever be until I died myself. God gave me the honor—and what an honor—to pass my partner to the waiting angel. This is an undeserved honor on my part. I was not worthy to be this close to heaven. It was a blessing beyond my power of understanding.

In the early morning hours of 9-11, I could see my reflection in the window of the hospital where I stood signing papers the nurse put in front of me. *Oh my God, where do I go from here?* I could also see the silhouette of my husband in the reflection of the window, his soul now safely in heaven. He was free of pain, suffering, and the worries of this world. He had safely arrived on the other shore. He was assured of that by the choice to follow God years before.

The head nurse asked everyone to leave the room so they could to prepare Glenn's body for transport. The room was empty for the first time all night. Glenn's brother Donald, Pastor Pat, and I were all that remained. They explained his wedding ring would need to come off, and Pat said he would get it; Donald said he would as well. But it only seemed right for me to remove it; after all, I was the one who put it on him to begin with.

I made my way to the left side of the bed and gently lifted the hospital blanket to expose his left hand. I slid my hand under his, gently lifted his hand, and carefully removed the wedding band, as not to hurt him or disrupt him. Under the covers, his body was still warm—so warm for a split second I was tempted to curl up next to him. The warmth was the kind that makes you feel safe and cozy when you are beside it. I had felt that warmth from him so many times before. I knew though that the warmth wouldn't stay this time. This was it. It ended the way it had started years before; the cycle was complete. Till death do us part.

ZZZZZ

8

The Funeral

THINGS seemed to move rather quickly after I signed my name on the final paperwork. It was late and the very thought of walking back down the corridor I had days prior made my limbs go weak. I couldn't do it. After everything I had to do that day, from telling Glenn it was okay to leave to removing the wedding ring I had placed on his finger years before, walking down the hall seemed like a feat too harrowing to take on.

"I can't," I whispered at the doorway.

"Why don't we go out the back way?" Terry suggested. I nodded. It felt like I had been pardoned from a death sentence.

The back was through a small door, down one flight of stairs. I followed Terry through the maze of backrooms that patients don't ever see. We made our way through what looked like the laundry room and eventually to a door that dropped us right outside the emergency room. The kids, everyone from Church, friends that had stayed with me all day—we all walked together silently in the bowels of the hospital until we reached the door. I thanked Terry for everything. She only hugged me in response. She was experienced in what a grieving widow needed.

Outside everyone chattered amongst themselves about where they would go. Usually I was the one organizing. On any other day, I would already have everything planned out, and most would be coming to our house, where I'd have fresh linens on the bed and a giant meal ready for visitors. I was the planner—the one who always knew what was going to happen next. where everyone was going to spend the night. Entertaining had always been one of my favorite pastimes. That night I didn't concern myself about where others would go or what they would eat when they got there. I had no idea what my house looked like, and if there was food in the fridge, it was sparse. None of that mattered though. I just wanted to go home. I wanted to collapse and worry about no one but myself. I had never felt that before. Grief does funny things.

As we stood in the pale yellow of security lights in the emergency room parking lot working out who would go where, a man appeared pushing a gurney. He was headed for a van parked off to my left. The person they pushed wasn't a patient. I knew because a white sheet covered the entire body. It was Glenn. They were carrying him away. My blood seemed to stop flowing for a split second.

We all stopped talking and watched as they loaded him into the back. The men that loaded him did it the way they might load a roll of carpet or a piece of furniture. They weren't careless with him, but the way they moved and the expressions on their faces didn't seem to match the task they did. My heart was breaking as I watched. Theirs weren't. Of course, I knew there was no reason for the men to feel as shattered as I did. They were just doing their jobs. They were respectful and worked quickly in cadence. To think that moving my husband's body was just someone's *job* though—that tore through me. I had wanted him to leave that hospital so badly every day for an entire month. I ached for the day we could say goodbye to the place. I never imagined he'd be leaving that way. He was supposed to be leaving with his arm wrapped around me, not with a white sheet covering him. He was supposed to go home with me in his big pick-up, not with two strangers in a coroner's van. None of it was right. None of it.

Everyone was quiet until the van disappeared into the dark of the night, but even when they started talking again, I heard nothing. All I could do was think about how alone I was. Glenn was my life, and a white van had just carried him away from me. My life as I knew it was over. I had no idea what I did next. How do you keep on living when half of you dies? The sound of Lacie crying shook me out of my head.

I looked at Lacie and realized that I had not yet thought about how hard this would be for her. I had lost my husband, but she lost her daddy, and never again would she share that special love between a daddy and his girl. It hit me that Glenn wouldn't be there to walk her down the aisle or see his first grandchild. Some of the happiest moments for Lacie would also serve as reminders that someone is missing. I squeezed Lacie's arm and she laid her head on my shoulder.

"Everything will be alright, somehow," I told her. I didn't believe it, but I was the leader of the group and I had to be tough. I looked over at the boys as I held Lacie. They had lost something irreplaceable too. They were silent, a silence so loud it was deafening. We were all lost.

That night when we finally got home, Lacie slept we me. I was so happy to have her there next to me in a bed that Glenn had slept in so many times. I don't know what I would've done if I would have had to sleep in it alone. Instead of sleeping, we talked. We talked and talked, and before I knew it the sun was shining through the open blinds. The worst night of my life had come and gone, but the experience was far from over. The rising of the sun meant it was time for me to go to the funeral home and start making decisions about what the service would be like and what kind of casket we would lay Glenn to rest in. For the first time, I wished that anybody but me was in charge. Suddenly I didn't want to control things or keep things going. I just wanted Glenn. If he were there, I told myself, I'd ask him to make the decisions for me.

God made the morning after Glenn's death a beautiful one. The air was crisp and smelled clean. Our little house felt good. It was so cozy, with the boys in their bedrooms and Lacie there. I knew as the sun poured in that we would soon all meet in the kitchen, where we'd sit together and have coffee, like we had so many times in the past. Quiet morning with the family were always my favorite. I knew, though, that that morning would not be the same. We were missing something—something vital, the centerpiece of it all. Glenn would not be there to tell Jonathan to get out of his chair or tell Logan to keep his fingers out of the Nutella. Lacie would not laugh at her dad or tease the boys with him. Those times were memories. We would only be able to talk about them.

The house buzzed with activity that morning. The boys were on their phones nonstop, calling friends to tell them what had happened. The phone never stopped ringing – people checking in on us or wanting to know what had happened. Then the doorbell started. Before we'd made it through a pot of coffee people were at our doorstep with casseroles and bagel trays and massive pans of pastries that were still steaming. I wondered if they stayed up all night cooking. Everything was fresh and looked wonderful. Instantly the house was filled with the smell of fresh cinnamon rolls, coffee, and breakfast casseroles.

As we finished breakfast, Glenn's family began to arrive to follow us to the funeral home. Together made the final arrangements. We decided to have it simple, because that is what Glenn would have wanted. It only seemed appropriate to have the service at the little church we had worked so hard building for so many years, so that is what we did.

The day of the funeral, the little church filled to capacity half an hour before the service was to start. I noticed the ushers setting up chairs outside on the porch. The church had never been that full before. I recognized most faces, but some I was sure I had never seen before. I didn't know whether or not to introduce myself. What is the proper thing to do in that situation? I had no idea, and really, I didn't care. What was important in that moment was that Glenn's dream of a packed house in that little church to hear God's word had come true. At all the committee meetings Glenn would reassure everyone that someday that little church would fill up. He promised! I wasn't happy about why it had come true, but I reminded myself that I wasn't in control anymore, and that God was doing His thing. I needed to sit back, listen and watch. That was something I had always had a hard time doing. Suddenly, I had no choice.

I looked around at how beautiful the church was that day. It was obvious a team of folks had worked the evening before cleaning and preparing. The wood shone and the concrete floor was spotless. Fresh flowers that had not been at the nursing home the day before were everywhere. The seat Glenn always sat in had a bundle of white flowers laying on it. No one would take his spot that day. His beautiful casket sat right up front, below the stage, the place he had stood thirty days before. Behind him there was a giant screen that would show pictures to remember Glenn. We had watched movies on the screen so many times during the church's movie night. That day, the main feature was Glenn. He lay there so peaceful with his Circle C Cowboy Church oxford shirt on. I knew he was rejoicing in Heaven at the crowd and the beauty of the day.

The service began with the same two songs we had sung as he was released to be with the Lord, "Precious Lord" and "Amazing Grace." The giant crowd sang together. It was so beautiful, and there were so many voices, I knew Glenn had to have heard us up in Heaven. After we finished the last chorus of "Amazing Grace," our pastor asked if anyone would like to speak. What followed is what this entire story is all about.

I was astonished at what happened after Pastor Pat called for any memories of Glenn. One by one, people all over the church raised their hands, stood up, and gave their own testimony about what Glenn meant to them. They talked about how he had helped them through hard times and what impact his words had on them when they were in their darkest moments. I didn't even know some of the people who shared stories of my husband with tears in their eyes. I assumed those I didn't know had worked with Glenn at Le Tourneau, where he had been a Supervisor for many years, but he never discussed any of stories with me.

At one point a young man stood up in the "balcony" section of the church that we rarely used. I looked up at a face I had never seen as the man talked from behind the chicken wire that enclosed the area to make sure no one fell from the makeshift mezzanine.

"Glenn was there for me when my wife left me and I felt like I had nothing left in the world," the man said, choking out the words. "He didn't have any idea what was going on. He thought I was just having a bad day, and he sat and talked to me to try to get my mind off things. I was thinking about killing myself that day, but I didn't because of Glenn. He didn't do anything real special. He just took the time to talk to a guy that was down. Just him talking to me gave me a new outlook. I guess you could say I owe Glenn my life."

I sat there in awe as I watched a rough around the edges man tear up talking about my husband. Another man stood up after that to share a similar story. People share how Glenn helped them get out of drugs, drinking, and bad relationships.

Among them was the man that Glenn used to smoke cigarettes with out in the driveway. When it was his turn, he told everyone in that jampacked church of all the times he and Glenn just sat on the tailgate of his truck and Glenn counceled him. I felt a sting of regret when I thought about the way I'd nag him for hanging out with someone I thought was a bad influence. It occurred to me in that moment that the man wasn't influencing Glenn; it had been the other way around. Glenn was showing him how to be a man—a good man. And he took my nagging because he knew that man's life was worth it. All that time I had thought we needed to be around our church group to be doing God's work, Glenn was doing it the way Jesus and the Apostles did, kicking rocks with people I thought might be drunks and deadbeats, showing them the way. I thought his recovery was our big story. His testimony had already been told, who knows how many times on the tailgate of a pickup. He didn't need a church to share God's love.

After almost an hour of people sharing their stories of Glenn, an older gentleman rose from his chair to speak. He worked with Glenn at Le Tourneau, I knew. He had been above the ranks from Glenn, and I remembered him because Glenn always said that, "Jim Frank scares me a little. He has a sharp tongue sometimes." It stayed with me because not much intimidated Glenn, but this man did. He stood up that day and said, "Are all you all listening to what has been said here today? Not once did someone talk about how big his house was or how nice his car was. Not once did someone say they would miss his parties or told stories of them drinking and acting crazy. All the stories are about this gracious, caring, godly man. These are the best things you can say about a person—not what they had or what stupid things they did."

He was sharp, just like Glenn had described, but also soft and tearful. It seemed the man that had intimidated Glenn held a great amount of respect and admiration for him because he saw who Glenn was.

It was like listening to people speak about a saint. *When was all this counseling happening?* I wondered. *Why did Glenn never share this with me?* I sat there listening to these stories with a broken spirit. How could I have been so judgmental of Glenn and his Christian witness?

I had been upset with him so many times because I thought he was being a terrible Christian example at work. I didn't think he concerned himself with sharing the gospel as much as he needed to. And then there were all the roughnecks he would spend too much time with in my opinion. He was doing it all wrong as far as I could see. I started to understand that day as we told Glenn goodbye that the miracle in this story was not the healing of Glenn's wounded body; the healing was happening in me. Glenn had lived his big story, every single day he went to work. He didn't need his body to be healed. What did needed healing was the way I saw my faith and others. Not only that, if I wasn't in control of something, I refused to believe it was the right way. From God to Glenn I had to be in control. Shame on me, again.

Renee our pastor's wife and my best friend, was the very last to speak. She made her way to the microphone. No one else had used the microphone, but she intended to be heard, inside the building and outside. So many folks outside.

"A great story I remember about my friend Glenn" she started. "The four of us went on a mission trip to Wyoming last year, and it was amazing—it was a vacation to us all as much as a mission trip I think. Well, except one day," she said and then paused a moment. "Pat and I had been the lead vehicle for most of the trip and when we left Cody, Wyoming to head out to Buffalo Bill's place, we asked Glenn and Kim to lead. No big deal," she said, smiling through her tears. "We were at the visitor's center and picked up the brochure for our next stop. We went back to our car as Kim gave Glenn the address to plug into their GPS system. Next stop, Pahaska Tepee Lodge. We followed them out of the parking lot, made a series of turns, and were right back in the visitor's center parking lot. We started again, drove around Cody, then right back to the center. What is going on?" Everyone laughed a little as Renee spoke. She told the story so well it was like watching a professional speaker.

"So, I call Kim and said, 'this is great; can you not get out of town? I feel like we have seen these sites enough.' I heard Glenn say, 'Oh no, she didn't just say that.' I could tell that he wasn't a happy camper. They had plugged the address in again, and same results. It just kept circling them around. I could tell it was getting ugly in the lead car. Glenn ended up pulling the GPS off the front window and throwing it at Kim. She was shocked he would do that, and he was furious. Come to find out later that evening when we met for dinner, Kim had been reading the address off the back of the brochure, which was the visitors' centers address, NOT the Pahaska Tepee Lodge address." Everyone laughed again, except for me. I couldn't figure out why she would tell THAT story of all the stories to tell about Glenn, especially after all the heartfelt stories others had told. That one just made Glenn look like he had a hot temper and me look crazy. "We laughed, everyone apologized, and great times were had by all," Renee concluded.

I remembered how awful a day that was. I cried the whole way to the lodge. I *could not* believe he had thrown a GPS box at me. But then I remembered how beautiful the sunset was as we drove down a country road that was full of switchbacks. The water was flowing right beside the road. The color was vivid all around us in the setting sun. There had been a small shower right as we were leaving the visitor center and three rainbows appeared in the sky. I wished I had been speaking to him at that moment because the whole ride was breathtaking, but no way, no how, was I going to talk to him after all that! My pride robbed me of a moment with Glenn. How many times had that happened?

After we arrived at the cabin, and were back after dinner, where I had put on my happy face for our friends, I chewed him out back at the room. I did it quietly because they were in the next cabin and the walls were paper thin. I didn't want them to hear who I really was. I pinched him so hard, it left a bruise. Tears burned my eyes as I thought of that moment. *Why,* I kept wondering, *did she had to share THAT moment? We had so many good times. Why that?*

Pat stood up at the podium and took the story from there. "We laugh at this story today, but have you really thought about why we were lost?" he asked the room. "Sure, we had plugged in the wrong address, so we were following the wrong directions. Our GPS, or Global Positioning System, was leading us in the wrong direction. We all have a GPS, maybe not the one you are thinking of, but what about your other GPS, your Godly Positioning System? Do you have the wrong address plugged in so you are always going in the wrong direction?" he asked. I knew right then he was talking to me. Or if he wasn't, God was.

"Maybe you go in circles and never reach your destination. If the address you have entered is the world and things of it, you very well may be going in circles, right back to the same drama you are hoping to leave behind. You will arrive at the same destination over and over. You are lost, just like we were in Wyoming. If you haven't, today I challenge you to enter God into your GPS system. I invite you to try it, see where the road will take you. You will find your path will be easy as you navigate through this life and your final destination will be Heaven. You will never be lost again. God will direct your every path in the right direction. The direction that leads to HIM."

All that happened in Cody that day in July 2009, came back to mean so much that day as we celebrated Glenn's life. God's precious design showed me how HE is in everything we say, everything we do, and every place we go. My heart was full of pride because that would have been exactly what Glenn would have said if he were able to address the crowd. Our argument, which seemed silly looking back but felt so serious in the moment, turned into a priceless moment for all of those in attendance that day.

We renewed our wedding vows on that trip in Jackson Hole, Wyoming. We had talked about it throughout the trip, and by the time we reached the beautiful city we had found a closeness that had been lost. Heck, we had the preacher with us, so why not? The town had several huge arches made of deer antlers, all of them breathtaking. Strands of clear lights ran through them so they illuminated the evening sky. I had never seen such beauty. We all agreed one of arches would be the place to renew our vows.

We shopped that day for a ring to symbolize our new commitment, our "Three in the Saddle" commitment from

Ecclesiastes 4:12: "A three stand cord is not easily broken," it says. This verse symbolizes Glenn, myself and most importantly, our God. Together we were strong. We found rings that were stainless steel with three stones in them. All three stones were native to that area, perfect to remember that great place. The stones glistened in the sun.

That evening was cool for July, about sixty degrees. The air smelled so fresh and clean. As the sun began to set, we made our way to the biggest arch in the city and began the ceremony. Pat must have been working on the service during the day, he delivered it so well. He spoke about "Three in the Saddle" being a forever commitment. Glenn and I both cried. I bet folks around town thought we were crazy, these four older people having a wedding ceremony all by themselves in the middle of town. That was a year before the funeral. Was God preparing us for the day a year prior?

My mind was so engrossed in that memory, I almost forgot what was happening around me. I blinked and there I was, though, sitting at my husband's funeral.

Months later I received an email from a Banker friend of mine that lives in Dallas, Texas. The email was very simple: "I changed the address in my GPS after your husband's service. My life is now on the right road." I felt an enormous amount of pride swell up in me, just knowing after he died, he was still touching people's life. I responded to his email quickly, telling him he had found the right roads, and if I could do anything to help guide him along, just let me know.

I check on him still today from time to time and sure enough he is traveling with the Lord, sharing his GPS testimony with others. Again, God allowed me to see a life that was changed because of Glenn's testimony. I put the right address in my GPS too. My heart still aches to think that Glenn isn't here with me to travel down the right roads, but because his funeral finally showed me what Glenn's life meant—to others and to me—I am able to put my faith in God and know that He—not Kim—is in control. I will never be driving around lost again, because of Glenn. He taught me upon his leaving what Three in the Saddle really meant, and what it is to truly seek God with all your heart. He taught me that God DOES work in mysterious ways, and that I might miss them if I keep trying to shove God into my box. He taught me that doing Jesus's work happens in driveways or after work in the parking lot as much as it does in the church, if not more. Mostly, he taught me that when you really do live your faith, you know that following a heart that follows Jesus is much more important than following your own plans.

XXXXX

Epilogue

Where I am Today

GOD has helped me pick up the pieces of my life and his spirit has encouraged me to share "our story" with you. This story is not meant to be sad; it is meant to inspire and challenge you to always be positive. Live every day to the fullest, and love unconditionally. It is also meant to show two types of love. One love is our love for the Lord and his love for you, his Bride. The second type is love for your partner. Your covenant for better or worse, sickness and health, till death do you part. My husband and I loved each other, not because it was so easy to do that, but because we made a covenant to stay together and we made The Lord our guiding light. I want to encourage you to invite Jesus into your heart, if you have never experienced the peace that passes all understanding, you will, after you accept the free invitation God offers.

God's grace has given me another opportunity to love. I am grateful for the journey I took to bring me to this spot. I now believe that everything happens in the right order and at the right time according to God's will. I would not be the mother, grandmother, child or wife I am today if this story was not written into my life by God's great design. It is difficult to show love if you haven't been shown the gift of love. God's love for us is huge. He loved me enough to give me 30 days to fall in love with my husband all over again. He gave us a glimpse of the two people he put together years past. Through his love he gently taught me to trust him and not to question his power. He gave Glenn a pain free passing into his kingdom and allowed me to release him to the Angel who carried him there. That was not the end of the story, however; it was a new beginning. I am now married to a wonderful man—a man I prayed God would help me let down lightly when our relationship first began. A man I would have missed had I not finally internalized the lessons that God taught me through Glenn—the lesson to let go of the reigns and really give them to God. I did that, against my natural instincts to flee, I put all my faith in God, moved myself out of the driver's seat, and because of that I found love again when I thought that might be impossible. Because of the lesson Glenn taught me, though, I was able to stop myself in my tracks and follow God's path instead of my own. Because of Glenn, I also knew how to enter a relationship—with God at the center. My husband. Richard, was new to the idea of God being a vital part of marriage, but several long talks and counseling sessions later, we are growing together in God. I am also always growing in God in my own, personal ways.

I offer my story to remind everyone never take even one moment for granted. Find that person you can share life with, but can also share your faith with and, eventually, death. Love them unconditionally every day. Lead with your heart. Be a warrior for that person. Put God first in everything you do because, as I learned—rather, what I was taught—God designed your portrait, and it is perfect and will stay that way by God's design, not your own. I had to learn the lesson from my husband, as he told his story over and over the day he went to heaven. He touched my life that day, and so many others'. I was proud to be there with him as this final chapter unfolded.

We are all guilty of thinking that marriage doesn't have to be "until death do you part" at times. If we had given up on our marriage every time it appeared not to be going our way, I wouldn't have this amazing journey to talk about now. The darkest part of the night is just before the dawn.

Because of every part of this story I was able to move on and love again, as you have read without as much reservation and less worry. Because really think about this, what do we have to worry about? In death I learned to live. Live, not just exist! The lesson learned is never to take even one moment for granted. God was working a miracle in me as he gently held us in his hands. The miracle came in a different form than I had expected. It wasn't a miraculous healing or a world tour telling this amazing healing story. It was Glenn showing me what faith looked like, even as he lay dying. It was me learning to really listen when God was speaking. It was a wake-up call to me. I was the story. Listen closely, be steadfast and true, and cling to the Lord. Choose to take action.

Life is precious, and you may breathe your last breath before you complete this book. Step out of the way and let God light the path. Commit or recommit your life to the Lord. He is always there waiting with his magic eraser to adjust all the spills.

I hope that my story has helped you see what it took me so long to see myself. I hope that, like me, you are able to learn from Glenn's grace and complete faith in God, even in what we all think of as the most terrifying of times—when we are faced with our own mortality. Glenn showed me what faith looks like in action; in his last moments, he showed me what kind of peace we can have if we let go of control and hand it over to God completely. He also taught me the lessons Jesus taught the Pharisees. Faith isn't about appearances. It isn't about knowing the rules or being able to cite the Bible. It sure isn't about exiling those we think are not as faithful as we are. Glenn taught me faith was about reflecting Jesus in the strangest of times. It was about taking time out to kick rocks from the tailgate of a truck when a kid showed up who felt his life was in shambles, even if that kid had never walked into a church. It was about letting go of worldly expectations and looking to God, even when things aren't going our way. I am still learning to handle life the way Glenn handled his physical death—I say physical because I know that Glenn's life did not end with his last breath. He merely went on to a new life—an eternal life. I will forever be grateful that I was able to stand by Glenn's side in life and in death; it was truly a spiritual experience—one that has forever changed me.

I am carrying Glenn and the faith he demonstrated with me still today; I am growing and always striving to enact that faith. We all got to come along for the ride. We each learned a lesson.

No matter where you are in life right now, know that you have a choice to make. It is never too late as long as you have a breath to breathe. It is never too late to give it to God, and once you do, there will be a burden that lifts from your shoulders. You're not just hanging on to control when you try to dictate life the way I did; you're hanging on to a heavy load that God is ready and willing to take. So unload your burden, hand over the reins, and get ready to ride with God. It's a ride like no other, and God is ready for you!

What is your life story?

CPSIA information can be obtained
at www.ICGtesting.com
Printed in the USA
BVOW08s1620150218
508096BV00001B/1/P